Being With Infants & Toddlers

A Curriculum that Works for Caregivers

Beverly A. Kovach, R.N., M.N.
Susan Patrick, M.Ed.
Laura J. Briley, Editor

LBK Publishing
Tulsa, Oklahoma

This book is available at special discount when purchased in bulk.
Contact lbriley5@gmail.com or susan.patrick@cox.net or by writing to
LBK Publishing, 3031 South Trenton, Tulsa, Ok. 74114 USA or
FAX: 918-747-1837 for details.

Book design by Lyman Page
Cover photography by Jenny White Photography

A percentage of the proceeds of this book will be given for the continuation of Pikler training and research.

infants

Toddlers

When Laura Briley, President of Tulsa Day Schools hired me as a consultant to her child development centers, this book became a reality. Although I had a strong mentoring relationship with Laura's staff through several consultations and trainings, I felt the need for the staff to have a written guide they could readily access and reference. My inspiration in writing a curriculum for infant-toddler caregivers came after many years of working with and training caregivers involved in center care. As a previous childcare owner-director (in the late 1970's), my interest was drawn to assist my caregivers in their daily care and handling of the young child. In those days, many caregivers suffered from low esteem because they were unaware of their significance in the lives of the children and their families. I learned during those experiences how exhausting caring for infants and toddlers can be with long hours and limited resources. I began to understand how important the caregiver is in the lives of our youngest citizens. We now know that caregivers significantly shape how relationships form and and help determine the success of infant-toddler future relationships second only to their parents.

Beverly Kovach

I also learned from working with caregivers that there was a lack of a congruent philosophy of care within the structure of the center. There was a large discrepancy between caregivers about what constituted good practice. The philosophy depended on the individual beliefs of each caregiver. Therefore, what occured in the infant room may have little curricular relevance in the toddler room. This led to much confusion and chaos among the staff as to what should be best practice for infants and toddlers.

It wasn't until I met my mentor, Magda Gerber, and began training with her in 1986 that I was able to guide my caregivers into a philosophy of respectful and responsive caregiving within the framework of a mutually satisfying relationship. As I began training other child care workers, I identified that what the caregivers in my center had experienced was the norm for caregivers across the country.

I saw a need from listening to caregivers during workshops, to develop a curriculum guide for infant-toddler care that defined a philosophy and an approach based on what is developmentally appropriate for infants and toddlers. It is written for the caregiver to have a "how to" quick reference that defines appropriate practices. This curriculum includes the child in the care process and fosters competence and independence for each child's level of ability. After writing the book Being With Babies in 2008, , there was a need to expand the curriculum to toddlerhood, a very difficult stage to work with especially in center care. The curriculum guide includes but is not limited to Magda Gerber's Philosophy, The Pikler Approach, Erikson's Stages of Psychosocial Development and the philosophy of Maria Montessori.

I continue to be inspired by my mentor, Magda Gerber, founder of RIE™, the trainings of Anna Tardos, Director of the Pikler Institute, and the many caregivers who devote their time and service to infants, toddlers, and their families.

I am honored to have been a small part of this project. The work that has been done on this book is just a tiny portion of all the wonderful things that pioneers such as Dr. Emmi Pikler and Magda Gerber have sent out into the world. Just four years ago I was first introduced to the ideas of Magda Gerber through the work of Janet Gonzales-Mena and under the tutelage of Dr. Denise DaRosVoseles. For the last two years, I have been able to literally sit at the feet of Anna Tardos(Dr. Pikler's daughter) and tried to absorb at least a part of the wisdom and spirit that created the Pikler Institute. I have been in close collaboration with Laura Briley and Beverly Kovach as we tried to build our own little Pikler inspired place for children in Tulsa, Oklahoma. The innovative and dedicated work of Laura and Beverly has created a sense of community here, and I appreciate each of them for including me in bringing their dream to fruition.

Susan Patrick

Over the past 25 years, my life has been dedicated to being with children. I have been a nanny, a parent, a volunteer, a teacher, an administrator, and a daily learner. The knowledge that is passed along in this book would have been helpful to me in each of those stages of my life as an educator and it will be a valuable resource in any relation based infant toddler program. My dream is to continue to learn and grow in the Pikler Approach in order to pass along the true joy of being with each other to educators who influence the daily lives of children. It is with that dream in heart and mind that we embark on our next project to provide a training and research facility for those in the U.S. who want to learn more about the work that Dr. Emmi Pikler began in Hungary so many years ago.

Susan Patrick is a PhD student at the University of Oklahoma and the Education and Program Manager at Day Schools Child Development Centers in Tulsa, Oklahoma. She presents on infant and toddler topics at local and national conferences and is an adjunct professor for Northeastern State University.

This book has been written because of our passion to share what we believe are best practices for infants and toddlers. An individual meets many people throughout their life and Beverly and I have been fortunate to meet some inspiring infant and toddler pioneers. It is important to honor and recognize the work of Dr. Emmi Pikler, Dr. Judit Falk, Anna Tardos, Magda Gerber, and Dr. Agnes Szanto whose roots began in Hungary. However, their scientific research and knowledge of infants and toddlers has spread throughout the world.

Laura Briley

I met Anna Tardos at the Pikler Institute in Budapest, Hungary in 1992 after establishing a pre-school in an orphanage in Romania. The work she was doing at The Pikler Institute showed me the dramatic difference between custodial care and relation based care. The importance of "respect" and treating the child as an individual was unheard of in most orphanages. My first trip to Hungary led to 12 more inspirational visits. The Pikler/Loczy Fund USA (PLUSA) was established. It became my personal mission to share this approach with others. We have organized Pikler trainings in the United States and have taken groups to the Pikler Institute. We have also established the Working Group for Children's Rights in Children's Homes in association with the World Forum Foundation.

It has been my good fortune to be associated with Beverly Kovach who has been an inspiration to caregivers. Her teaching style is unparalleled. She makes the philosophy easy to understand and is an expert in relation based care. She has provided countless hours of training and consulting to improve my own school's learning environments. She and Susan Patrick have collaborated and worked side by side in the classroom with the caregivers mentoring and supporting them. She has shared her knowledge with Susan and they have written a book for caregivers that puts theory and philosophy into daily practice.

The majority of the photos were taken at Day Schools and we would like to thank those families who allowed us to photograph their baby, and thanks to the following Day Schools' faculty: Jacci Townsell, Celeste Dunigan, Sasha Reedy, Stephanie Wills, Colleen Walling, Joyce Maissell, Teri Myers, Jaci Hopkins, Tammy Ogle, Julie Verdeja and Patty Harjo. There are many people who have been an inspiration for us in collaborating on this book. We give special thanks to our families, Bonnie and Roger Neugebauer, Community Playthings, and PLUSA board members: Alexandra Curtis-Boyer, Elsa Chahin, Janet Gonzalez-Mena, Johanna Herwitz, Agnes Szanto, Intisar Shareef and Denise Da Ros Vosales.

We are reaching out to those individuals who want to learn more about "being with infants and toddlers". Our goal and vision is to make quality infant care accessible to children of all nations.

Pikler Methodological Institute,
Budapest, Hungary

Anna Tardos

Anna Tardos was the last Director of the Pikler Institute in Budapest, Hungary and child psychologist. She currently holds the position of President of the Pikler-Loczy Association, Hungary. For over 50 years she has conducted research on self-initiated free movement and play activity of infants and toddlers. She travels throughout the world lecturing and providing training to professionals. She has published 60 articles in five languages and is author, co-author and editor of several books, videos, and curriculum on infants and toddlers. She is an honorary member of the French World Mental Health Association.

She has been our mentor and friend for many years. She has always challenged our thinking and assisted us as we work with infants and toddlers and professionals. Her insight into the world of the baby is based on her life's work and the influence of her mother, Dr. Emmi Pikler. It is our honor to know her.

Laura, Beverly, & Susan

History

The Pikler Institute (nicknamed Lóczy from the street where it is located), was established in 1946 by pediatrician Dr. Emmi Pikler. The City of Budapest commissioned Dr. Pikler to organize a home for infants and young children who were deprived of their parents until satisfactory living arrangements could be found.

The Pikler Approach is based on Dr. Emmi Pikler's research into gross motor development and emphasizes treating babies with respect by valuing self-initiated activity, building trusting relationships between child and caregiver, sustaining each child in building self-awareness, and fostering optimal health. It is said in Budapest that "Pikler babies" can be recognized even when they are older because they move with grace and freedom. Dr Pikler believed that this is because they were allowed to move naturally and at will and allowed to spontaneously follow their own in-born developmental time table.

Dr. Emmi Pikler, Budapest, Hungary

Magda Gerber, a pioneer in the field of infant and toddler care in the United States is noted for her work with parents and professionals who have or work with infants and toddlers. She was the Founder of RIE™, Resources for Infant Educarers, in Los Angeles, California.

Her underlying message was to provide care and respect especially during caregiving times, like diapering, bathing, dressing, etc. During these "fully there" engaged times together, both the young child and adult become socially and emotionally fulfilled.

Magda Gerber believed it was possible to allow infants and toddlers to move freely and play with objects of their choice in a safe environment without much adult intervention because of their rich relation based caregiving times.

Her mentor and long time friend was Dr. Emmi Pikler. Dr Pikler was her pediatrician and mentor before coming to the United States.

Magda Gerber, RIE Founder

Philosophy for Infant Caregiving

Quality infant caregiving is based on respectful and responsive relation-based care by the adult through sensitive observation of the infant. Through sensitive observation, the adult is able to read important cues from the infant. Infant cues are valuable in order to meet the needs of infants accurately and in a timely fashion.

When the adult spends focused time with the infant during caregiving routines, a special relationship deepens attachment between the primary caregiver and the infant. These daily predictable experiences rich in language, promote a dialogue specific to the process occurring between the caregiver and infant. Repeated experiences fuel cognition, understanding, cooperation, and language, as well as social-emotional competence of the infant. When infants needs are met and fueled on these developmental domains, infants become content. Infants who are nurtured and satisfied, play with objects and others more peacefully and productively.

Contented babies are able to concentrate, explore, and demonstrate curiosity in the world around them. Through self initiated movement, infants are able to gain balance on their own without the use of artificial props. As they move and explore, they are able to choose objects of their own interest. Children are grouped according to their abilities and development, this maintains safety in peer-peer interactions.

The rationale and basis for the care process is based on Magda Gerber's philosophy of respect for infants and the Pikler Approach to quality infant care in group settings. The Pikler Approach has research documenting infant ability to become autonomous and competent in group settings.

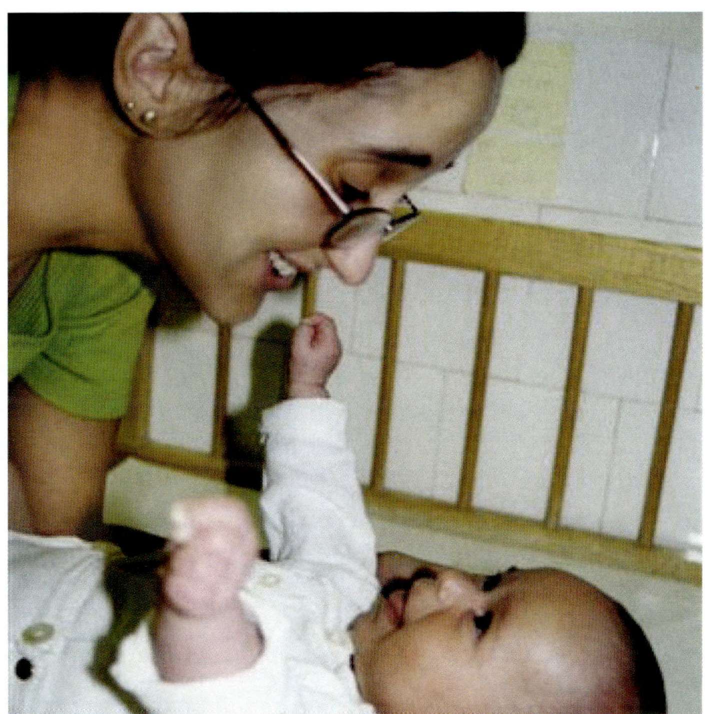

Pikler Institute
Budapest, Hungary

When developing curriculum and environments based on the growing needs of infants, it is important to follow the Standards for Developmentally Appropriate Practice developed by the National Association for the Education of Young Children (NAEYC), as well as your federal, state, and local guidelines.

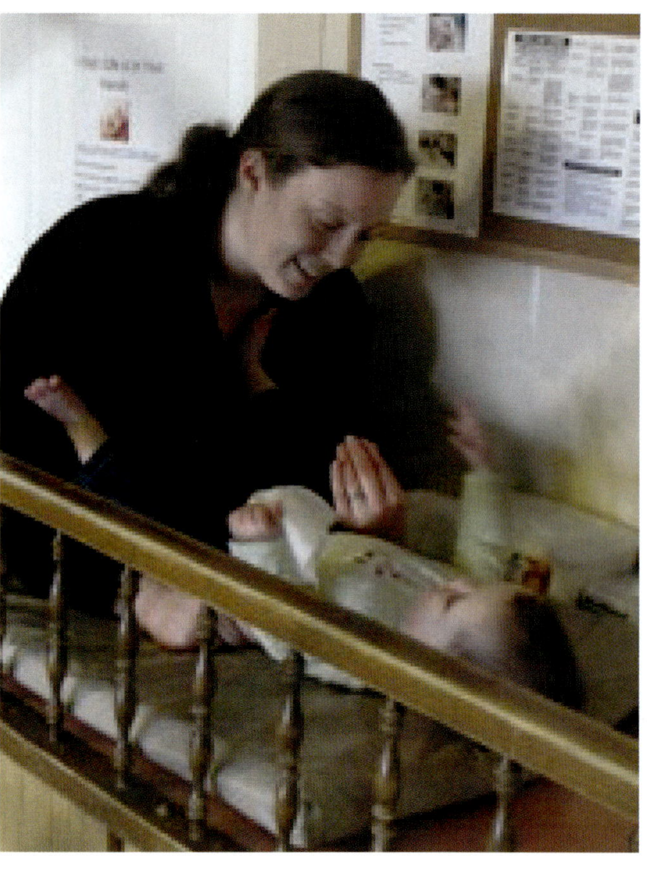

Caregiving Curriculum

Relate

The caregiving relationship between you and the baby during feeding, diapering, and sleep is the Curriculum. This relationship provides the foundation by which a special person learns through repeated experiences to know and understand each particular baby's needs and wants. The baby then begins to trust in the caregiver's ability to understand him as a person. This is called Primary Care.

Observe

Observation is a skill that needs practice to acquire. To observe accurately, the adult needs to sit quietly and concentrate on the baby's behavior and actions. This can be done briefly and often throughout the day. By slowing down, you will be able to observe and read the baby's cues more accurately. Slowing down helps to give the baby time to process what is happening.

Read

Reading babies' signals helps you to understand what the baby is trying to say. These cues are important information needed in order to give responsive and accurate care. For example, crying, yawning, and rubbing of eyes tell you the baby is probably getting tired and ready for nap.

Respond

Respond to what you see happening with the baby. Go to the baby reporting what you see using descriptive language: "I see you are yawning, and may be tired. I am going to pick you up and put you in your bed to sleep." Extend your arms and wait for his reaction. This will give the baby time to react to you and what he understands is happening.

Wait

Wait for the baby to respond to you. Include his response in your next reaction to him. Perhaps he is ready to be picked up. You see him wiggle his arms and legs, then respond by telling the baby what you see happening: "Oh, I see you are ready for me to pick you up." This reflection and feedback helps the baby to understand and comprehend more clearly what is happening.

Including Baby in His/Her Care

Many people who work with babies feel they must do something for the baby in order for the baby to be satisfied. What happens when the adult "does for" the baby is that the adult often forgets to include the baby in the caregiving process. The attitude about caregiving "for" infants originates in the belief system of adults that babies are helpless and totally dependent on adults for their care. Often adults believe that babies are not yet ready to understand what is happening to them. From this point of view, including or excluding the baby in his care makes little difference.

In child care centers, the belief about baby "helplessness" continues. The adult who provides the baby with his physical routines of care neglects including the baby in the caregiving process. The effect is the baby is "acted upon" rather than "with" the adult when receiving care. This attitude leads to automated care. Automated care means care that is so basic and repetitive that one does not have to think before acting. The danger in giving care to infants in a take-for-granted manner is that the baby gets the message that he is an object instead of a unique individual.

We need to stop and take a look at what happens to a baby who receives care that does not include him. Adults respond to a baby's cry by being anxious about the crying baby. Because of their anxiety, adults often respond too quickly to the crying baby without observing or thinking about why the baby is crying. Instead, we try to get the baby to stop crying. This quick reaction leads the adult to try to meet the needs of the baby based on what the adult assumes the baby needs at that particular time. By reacting in haste, we forget to include the baby in his care and leave out important cues from the baby that can give more accurate and authentic care.

Most adults do not consider a baby's cry as a form of communication. When and how a baby cries tells us important information. Developing a "third ear" (sensitive observation) will help the adult in reacting more specifically to why the baby might be crying.

Listed below are helpful caregiving hints that include the baby in his or her care:

1. Observe the baby before reacting. By observing the baby, you can give more accurate care. Why is the baby crying? Is he wet? When did he last eat? Is he tired? Did something frighten him? These types of questions need to be part of how you think before offering assistance to the baby.
2. Talk to the baby about what you are about to do for him/her. By telling the baby what you are going to do before you do it, you give the baby a cue or warning that something is going to happen to him. Isn't this a more respectful way to be with a baby you are caring for? Language helps the baby begin to understand what it is that the adult is about to do and also helps in the development of speech.

Including Baby in His/her Care

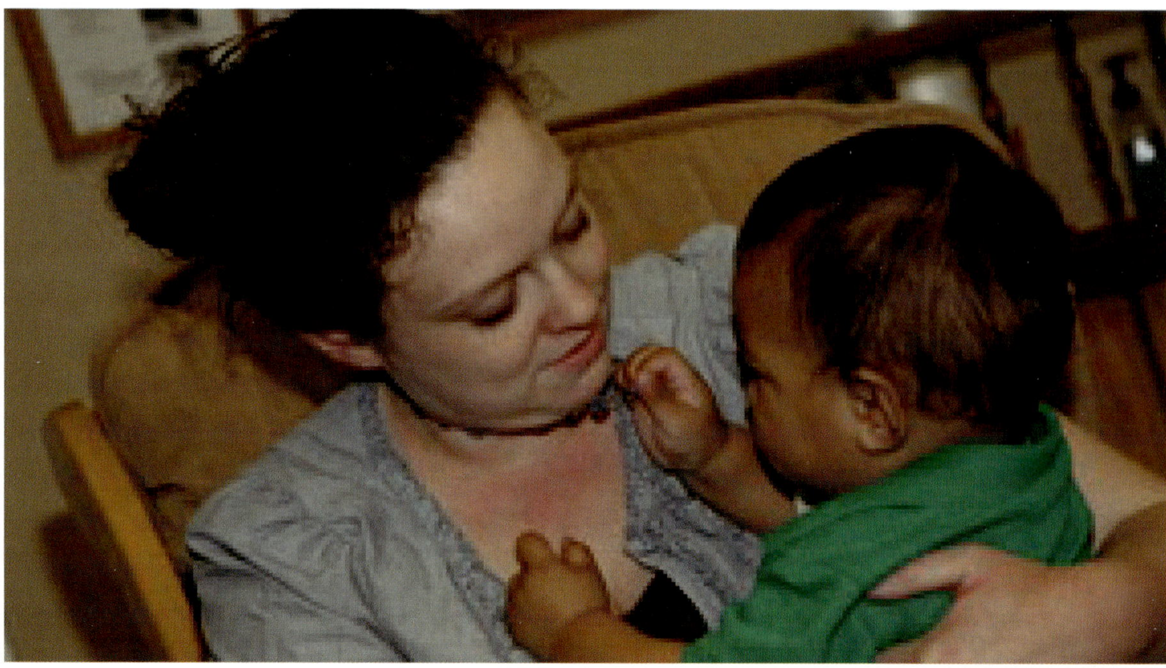

3. When giving care to the baby, give undivided attention. Being "fully there" during physical care offers the baby time that is just for him. What better way to let the baby know how special he is? And to do so without any outside interruptions would be very special indeed.
4. Provide a safe place for baby to move about freely. Babies need lots of time to explore and play. Freedom of movement unrestricted by contraptions offers the best learning environment for baby to grow and develop.
5. Provide a peaceful mealtime for baby free from interruptions. Hold the baby while feeding.
6. Talk to the baby during burp times.
7. Let the baby eat or not eat at his own pace. Do not rush feeding. Feeding needs to be an enjoyable experience where the baby has a choice in how much to eat. Think, is this how I would want to be cared for if I was that baby? Asking yourself that question will help you in providing sensitive and individual care.

By being fully there for baby, your presence is saying "you are special". Following these simple suggestions will influence how the baby feels about his world. You will have helped him understand his world better because you have included him in his care.

Your Relationship with the Baby is the Curriculum

Authored by: Beverly Kovach & Denise Da Ros-Voseles

You are the caregiver who works in the infant room of a center-based facility. You experience many interruptions throughout the day: parents coming in and out, telephones ringing, staff wanting to bend your ear about their latest problem, as well as those crying babies. You can easily see how numerous interruptions contribute to you and the baby being over stimulated. So how are you going to keep all of those babies content and on schedule?

Well you probably are not, which can eventually be in the best interest of the baby.

More often than not, infants in group care do not have the luxury of being cared for based on their individual needs. Too often, rigid room schedules are followed, making babies eat and sleep when adults say they are ready. This may happen at the center you work in. If it does, the curriculum is not centered on the baby being first priority. We need to remember why we are here. We're here for the baby. The baby is the curriculum. But, in your everyday work situation, it's a struggle to keep the baby as the primary focus of your day.

Let's think about those babies you care for on an everyday basis. Obviously, it is an uphill battle to see each baby at your center as an individual in a way that allows him/her to receive timely and tuned in care. The scene described earlier with all those interruptions does not lend itself to a relationship rich in observation and caregiving of individual babies.

What would it take for the baby to get his specific needs met? First, as infant caregivers, we would need to believe and see that the baby is the primary focus of each day. We would need to believe in our heart and act in ways that support each baby's own sense of what he/she needs. And we would have to believe that what we do with babies makes a difference in their lives.

"Madeline, you look like you are getting tired. I saw you yawn and rub your eyes. Let me take you from the playroom and see about changing your diaper before nap." Latisha's observation was very accurate as Madeline soon fell asleep in the safety and comfort of her crib.

Keeping the focus individualized based on each baby requires alert observation and timely accurate action. This is very hard to do in group care. And yet, for babies to thrive and survive physically and emotionally, it needs to happen.

Let's look at what is meant by "you and the baby as the curriculum." This means that because the baby comes first, you, the caregiver, have to develop a meaningful and special relationship and bond with that baby. The baby has to know you and feel comfortable enough with you in order to allow you to care for him/her. This relationship is built on an understanding between you and the baby as to what it is the baby needs and wants at a particular time. This kind of knowing the baby takes quite an investment on your part; an investment built on time. Time needed to relate and build a relationship together that is grounded in trust. Some key elements essential for you to develop a trusting relationship with the babies you care for and about include:

- Observe what is happening with the whole child.
- Provide a safe, calm, peaceful environment.
- Give one-to-one individualized attention.
- Stay focused on the baby.
- Create constant routines of care.
- Provide choice and options that support baby's preference.
- Include the baby in caregiving.
- Talk with the baby about what is happening.
- Provide responsive and respectful caregiving.
- Wait for the baby to respond and include that response in your next action with the baby.

Feeling and responding to babies in respectful ways requires you to accept and incorporate these behaviors into your caregiving relationship. Start today. Pick one thing you are going to try while you care for your babies. This is a beginning point for you to start to include some of these measures in your caregiving with your baby.

Perhaps you have already been thinking about babies in this way. If not, it may be time for you to start by doing one thing differently with the babies in your care. Perhaps deciding to greet each baby by name every morning is a great first beginning to individual acknowledgement. The way you treat and handle babies will eventually affect how special each baby feels about himself in the future.

Your hands can be the messenger that tells the baby that he/she is special. For instance, when moving a baby from one place to another, your hands tell the baby he/she is respected and special by the way you gently and securely hold him/her.

This gentle and careful handling of the baby will help you develop a special regard for all babies you care for and about. Respectful handling and holding of the baby gives him/her the message he/she is important. These are the babies that will come to have higher regard for themselves; an attitude that each baby needs for social and emotional health to flourish.

Since you're one of the important ingredients in developing a relationship with the baby, you'll need to explore "how" you're going to be with infants in your care. Relax; it doesn't have to be that hard a task. While your baby is awake and in need of care, like feeding or being diapered, it's the best time to build a relationship and have a presence together. Paying full attention to that baby, trying to understand what the baby needs, and including the baby in his/her care gives an important message to the baby. A message that says he/she is special, worthy and deserving of getting his/her needs met. Magda Gerber often said, "paying attention to the baby is the single

most important thing you can do that lets the baby know he/she is unique and very special." Below is an example of providing that special action that can make a difference for the baby.

Keri loves feeding Noah his bottle. He is eager and responsive in his sucking. She found through repeatedly feeding Noah that he likes his milk slightly warmed. Noah sucks harder and tugs at his fingers when the temperature of his milk is just right. Keri makes a point of always having the temperature of his milk just right for Noah. Keri's subtle message to Noah says, "you're important and special enough to give you your bottle the way you prefer."

If we believe the baby is the curriculum, our energy will be directed in spending time to know, to understand, and to be available to meet each baby's unique and individual needs. Knowing when and what to do for each baby at a particular time requires observation and many encounters with each baby in order to understand what the baby is trying to say.

- Babies need opportunities for peaceful alone time to explore.
- Babies need to be included in the caregiving process.
- Babies need opportunities to move freely and safely.
- Babies need sensitive and individualized care by a significant adult.
- Babies in group care need to experience how to solve their problems during some of their "struggles".
- Babies need to be allowed to interact with other babies in the same stage of development.
- Babies physical needs should be met on his/her own body's schedule, not a room schedule.
- Babies in group care need to be observed to try to understand what is best for them at a given time.

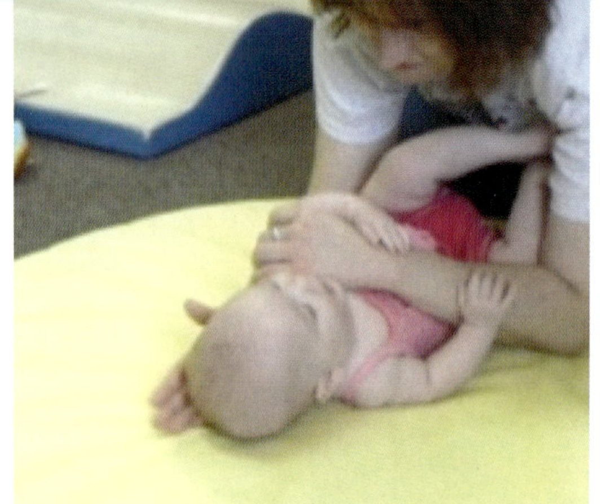

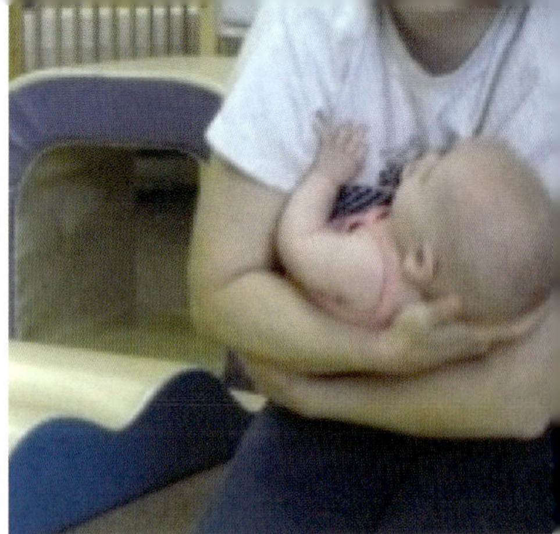

You make a difference in the lives of babies who are in group care by how you relate to each of them during those special caregiving times. Respectful and responsive caregiving is not an easy task to try to accomplish in group care. However, it is at the very core of fostering trust and mutual satisfaction between you and the baby. "Watching, asking, and adapting are the tools of responsive caregiving." (Lally, Griffin, Fenichel, Segal, Szanton, & Weissbourd, 1995, p35) Babies in group care tend to thrive in relationships where they are included in their caregiving process by a responsive and emotionally involved adult. Will that adult be you?

Caregiving Routines

Rationale:

During caregiving times, the baby and the adult caregiver have a chance to form a relationship together that is socially and emotionally rich. These physical care times happen frequently and can offer the baby and the adult meaningful and naturally satisfying experiences.

Routines need to:

- Be based on the baby's individual needs
- Be consistent
- Have rich language expression
- Provide time to allow the baby to participate
- Respond to cues from the baby
- Be enjoyable

Goals:

- To provide predictable experiences for the baby to learn what to expect
- To support a mutual relationship with the baby and the caregiver rich in language cues and responses
- To give time for the baby to cooperate and participate for his level of development

Process:

When you diaper, feed, dress, or nap a baby, understand each individual baby's preference. Your caregiving needs to reflect his or her individual needs and responses. Following a predictable routine during care helps the baby to understand what is about to happen. This consistency will help him to trust you as his caregiver.

Day Schools

Your Hands

When approaching an infant, be sure to slowly show the infant your hands prior to picking up the infant. Each infant needs time to process the information about what is going to happen. Allowing this time lets the infant know that you respect his need and cues him as to what will happen. This should occur each time you are about to do something with the infant (like diaper, feed, dress, etc). Being consistent with the infant helps them begin to understand what is about to happen.

Hands portray peace or violence, peaceful hands demonstrate care and respect to the infant. Your hands should be the first act of kindness and gentleness that the infant receives. Through your hands, the infant begins to feel his worth and learns to trust the adult who cares for him.

Procedure for holding an infant:

1. Go to baby and speak gently about what you are about to do - wait 5 seconds to give the baby time to process the language.
2. Make eye contact.
3. Bend toward the baby.
4. Move slowly and wait for the baby's response.
5. Place left hand over the left shoulder joint of baby and slide right hand down the back of the head, neck and spine.
6. Slide left hand under right hand and arm for support.
7. Lift forward, cradle and lift baby to your body.

A word about hands from Dr. Emmi Pikler

An excerpt from *Peaceful Babies-Contented Mothers*

Getting to know each other is, of course, mutual.

As we get to know the child, he begins to get to know us, and this happens primarily through our hands.

Hands constitute the first relationship for the baby with the world beyond breast feeding.

Hands pick him up, lay him down, wash, dress, and feed him.

What kind of world reveals itself to an infant?

What a difference it makes when gentle, patient, and peaceful hands, which also convey safety and clarity, take care of him.

How different the world seems if these hands are impatient, rough, hasty, restless and nervous.

In the beginning, hands are everything for the infant. They are the person, the world...

No matter how small he may be, we never treat a child mechanically as though he were an inanimate object.

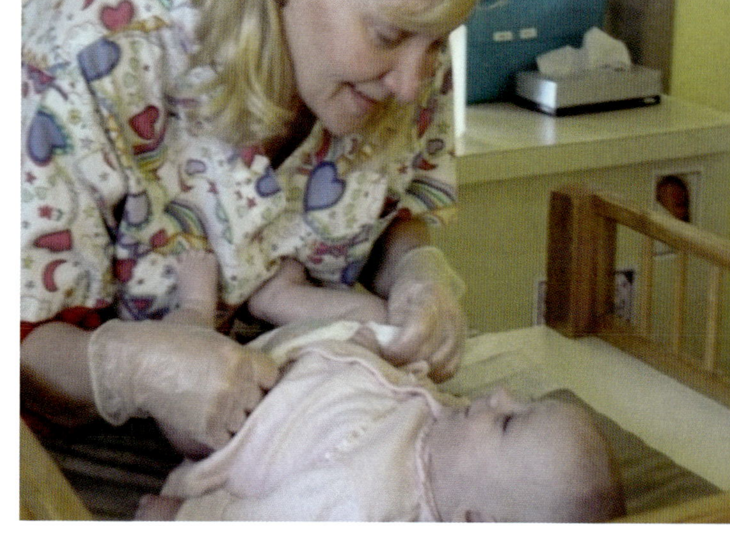

Diapering

Rationale:

Diapering is a routine that can enrich your relationship with the babies in your care. Diapering is done several times a day and builds a sensitive and responsive relationship between the caregiver and the baby. Being fully available and telling the baby what is happening is vital to understanding. When the baby knows what to expect, he will eventually be able to participate in his care process. When you slow down, you are able to read important cues and signals from the baby. This helps you to respond more accurately to what the baby is trying to tell you. Avoid interruptions that interfere with the quality of the diapering relationship.

Refrain from hanging objects over the diapering area (i.e. mobiles, mirrors, etc.) which distract the infant from the caregiving relationship. Diapering is an intensely personal experience and the baby should invited to be fully involved in the process rather than distracted from it. The infant is learning about trust and becoming emotionally attached to the primary caregiver. A baby is diapered over 5,000 times during his or her lifetime. Diapering should be a relaxed, positive experience. Caregivers can enhance the experience by using positive words rather than referring to the diaper change as dirty, smelly, or messy. Dialoging with the baby about the diaper, the wipes, and the parts of the body that are being cleaned allows the baby to build language and knowledge about the process.

Goals:

- To be consistent
- To watch for important cues from the baby so you are able to respond to what you see happening
- To talk to the baby, telling the baby what is happening while diapering
- To be fully present during the one on one diapering process
- To ask the baby to participate
- To diaper away from high traffic areas
- To develop an efficient and effective diaper area

Process:

1. Check diaper area for needed items.
2. Wash your hands and tell the baby that it is time for a fresh diaper.
3. Hold the baby supporting the head, neck, and spine.
4. Gently place the baby on the changing table placing the feet down first.
5. Put gloves on allowing the baby to see and feel the different texture.
6. Slowly remove any clothing, giving time for the baby to process what is happening.
7. Include the baby in the caregiving process.

8. Refrain from pulling baby's legs up by the ankles. Place hand and arm underneath the back of the baby's knees saying "lift up" and wait for the baby's response.
9. Clean the left side of the genital area and discard wipe, repeat on the right side, then the center using a clean wipe. Be sure to check the back for any soiling.
10. Place soiled wipes in the soiled diaper, fold diaper and close tabs. Place diaper inside glove as you remove the glove. Place soiled diaper in a lidded diaper container.
11. Tell the baby you are going to slide the clean diaper under his bottom. Wait for his response and report what he shows you from his response (i.e. I see you lifting your legs, so I know you're ready).
12. Continue to:
    - Say what you are going to do
    - Observe
    - Wait for the baby to respond
    - Tell the baby what you see happening and
    - Reflect your observation to the baby.
13. Point to the baby's hand and tell him you want to wipe his hands. Wipe each hand with a wet cloth.
14. Offer your hands to the baby saying, "We are finished diapering. It is time to pick you up."
15. Support and lift the baby, putting him on his back in the play area or in his crib.
16. Tell the baby you are leaving to clean up the diaper area and wash your hands.
17. Move slowly to leave the baby.
18. Clean the diaper area and wash your hands.

Diapering Area

- Clean and void of any play objects
- Near a water source
- Needs a changing table and liner
- Away from high traffic areas
- Items need to be accessible for each baby (diapers, change of clothes, etc.)
- Lidded diaper container
- Necessary diapering items (i.e. gloves, plastic bags, wash cloths, wipes, paper towels, etc.)
- Hamper for soiled linens (i.e. washcloths)

The Importance of the Changing Table:

This diapering table allows the baby to lie comfortably on her back while able to reference the caregiver's face. By being "on face' together, the adult and infant are able to clearly see and respond to each other's cues providing a rich and meaningful diapering experience together. As the infant develops and becomes more mobile, she can move freely and safely without being restricted by the adult. The role of the adult when diapering is to accommodate the body movements of the infant which allows the two to still be engaged in their relationship.

Feeding

Rationale:

Babies in group care need to eat with a primary caregiver who they know. Often in group settings, they have many things that distract from quiet, peaceful time between caregiver and baby. Because of this, babies may not eat to full satisfaction. This may set up a pattern of babies eating less and more frequently. When this occurs, babies don't understand how much or how little they need to eat for their bodies to be fully satisfied.

Feeding each baby on the lap of the caregiver not only enhances the attachment between the baby and the caregiver, but also gives the caregiver the ability to feel the changes in the baby's body that indicate fullness. These changes might occur as the baby needs to burp or becomes full. When the baby is on the lap, it is easy to feel the subtle shift from content eating to discomfort.

Goals:

- To establish a relationship based on trust
- To have one primary person feed each baby in his/her group
- To let each baby eat to his own satisfaction
- To develop a quiet, efficient eating place away from high traffic areas
- To understand that eating is for nutrition
- To support baby's individual needs regarding how much to eat
- To provide a climate that supports pleasurable eating

Key Concepts:

1. Eating is for nourishment.
2. Eating should be sensory.
3. Eating should be pleasurable.
4. The baby should determine how much to eat (self regulation).
5. The baby determines the length of time he needs to eat.

Procedures for bottle feeding:

1. Develop designated eating places.
2. Prepare the bottle beforehand on a tray with a washcloth.
3. Label all bottles.
4. Show the bib to the baby saying, "It is time to eat." Put the bib on before picking up the baby.
5. Take the baby to the feeding area.
6. Heated bottles must be tested before feeding to insure proper heat distribution.
7. Wash your hands and the baby's hands.
8. Bottle feed the baby on the adult's lap.
9. Place the baby in your arm at a 45-degree angle.
10. Show the bottle to the baby.
11. Put the nipple on the bottom lip and wait for the baby to take the nipple inside his mouth.
12. Avoid rocking or talking unnecessarily.
13. Burp every 2-3 ounces for young infants every 3-4 ounces for older infants (see burping protocol).
14. Stay focused on the baby avoiding adult interruption or conversation.

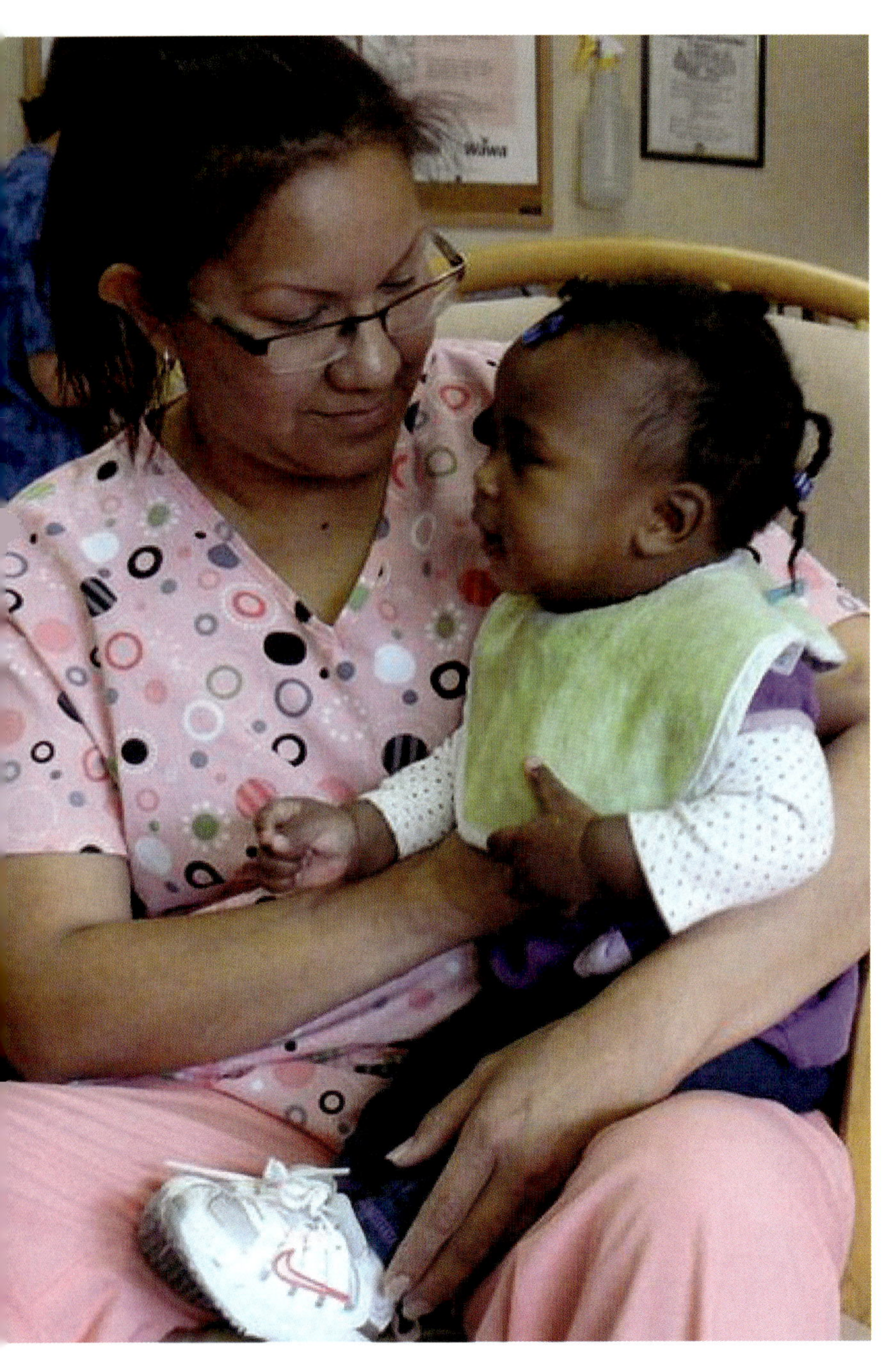

Burping Protocol

Often feeding babies appear so calm and peaceful until time to burp the baby. Many well meaning adults burp babies by tapping quite robustly several times on baby's back as the baby sits propped on the adult's lap. Imagine what the baby is feeling as his face is held by one of the adult's hands while she continues to drum on his back with the other. His face might show wide bulging eyes or an open mouthed grimace. The baby looks very uncomfortable and out of balance half suspended without support. The origins of this approach to burping, like rocking, must come from centuries of adults deciding what is best for babies. Babies will burp automatically, even difficult colicky babies if they are placed comfortably in an upright position against the body of the adult. Place baby upright against left side, keeping feet from touching lap. Remember the least amount of help for the baby to burp is always in the baby's best interest physiologically and psychologically.

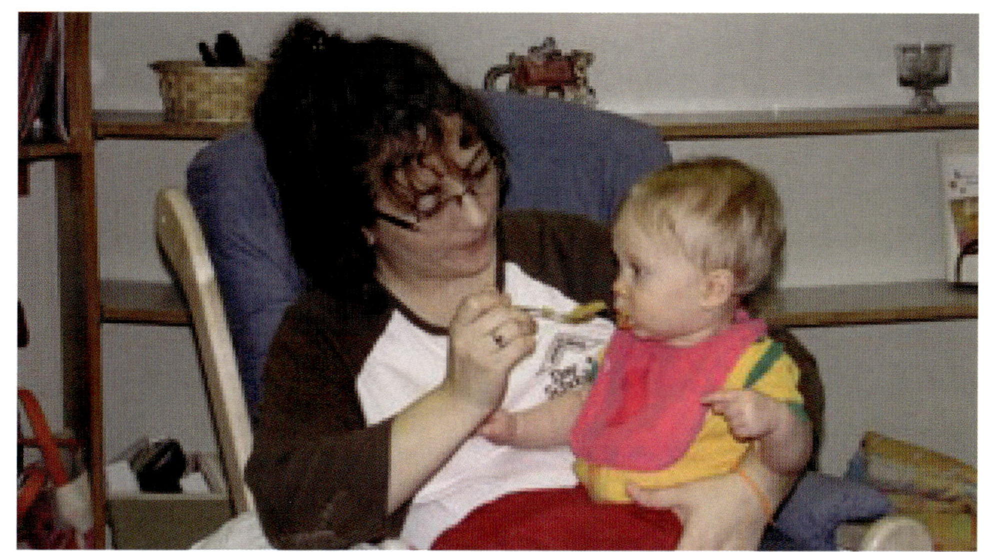

Process for eating solids:

1. Prepare solid food in a dish; place the dish on a tray with a spoon, washcloth, and a small glass of water.
2. Show the baby the bib saying: "I hear you are hungry, I have your food ready."
3. Place the bib on the baby before going to the eating area.
4. Go to the feeding area with the baby.
5. Slowly wash each hand with a washcloth.
6. Feed the baby on the lap at a 45-degree angle.
7. Offer food on a small spoon at eye level.
8. Bring food to the lower lip naming the food (i.e. "these are green beans").
9. When the baby gives you a cue he does not want more, stop feeding, saying "I think you are through eating."
10. Clean the baby's mouth and hands.
11. Remove the bib telling him that you are doing so.
12. Lap feed solids until the infant can support his head, neck, and upper trunk, and is able to sit up. He may then be offered to sit at a small child friendly table with a stool or small chair.

NOTE- Some children who are physically able to eat at a small table may not be emotionally ready to do so. Observe baby's signals and reactions to moving away from adult lap feeding to a more independent process (i.e. possibly wants to scoot off the lap of the caregiver).

Sleep

Rationale:

Babies need predictable rituals they can rely on for sleep. When babies are in group care, they may find it hard to fall asleep. Their routine may be different from what is done at home. Babies often have to adapt to different noises and people. A baby has to learn to adjust to many differences in order to be calm enough to fall asleep. When adults are sensitive to baby's sleep cues and respond to the baby's need for rest, the baby has a better chance to fall asleep in a group care setting.

Goals:

- To support each baby's sleep needs
- To allow babies to sleep in their own space
- To be consistent in routines when you put the baby to sleep

Key Concepts:

1. Watch for signs that tell you the baby is getting tired.
2. Approach the baby telling him you are going to put him in his bed.
3. Securely lift the baby, supporting his head, neck, and spine.
4. Place him in his crib on his back.
5. Cover the baby loosely, tucking the blanket in the sides of the crib. (depending on temperature).
6. Say "goodnight" and move away from his crib.

Note:

If difficulties arise with the sleep procedure, ask the parents what routines for sleep work. Babies who have learned poor sleep habits may need assistance. Sometimes putting your hand lightly on the baby's chest is helpful. If the baby is awake or cries in his crib for more than five minutes, or his cry begins to sound desperate, you may need to pick up the baby and try later. Some babies wake up during sleep. Try to give the least amount of help in offering assistance. The baby will often fall back to finish his sleep.

✔ **Watch for cues that the baby is tired and place him in the crib before he falls asleep. Babies should not fall asleep in the arms of an adult or in play areas.**

Place the baby on his back in his crib. Keep blanket away from baby's face by tucking it in at the bottom.

Signs of Sleepiness:

- Yawns
- Rubs eyes
- Cries
- Tired or red eyes
- Becomes inactive
- Begins to suck finger or fist

Adult Response:

Try to maintain a matter of fact attitude that the baby needs to rest:

- Believe and trust that the baby can self-regulate and learn to sleep on his own.
- Decrease stimulation.
- Develop a predictable sleep routine.
- Use a soft tone of voice and slow body movements.
- Respond minimally during initial sleep cycle.

Crying

Rationale:

Babies cry for many different reasons and it is a form of communication. Helping babies to understand their different cries is part of the adult role. Responding to baby's cry tells baby he has been heard and provides tuned in and sensitive care.

Goals:

- To try and understand the meaning of the baby's cry
- To meet the needs of the baby's communication in a timely fashion

Process:

A baby's cry is trying to tell you that he or she has a need. When caregivers observe first and try to understand what the baby is trying to say, there is a better chance that the baby's cry will be accurately understood. There are many reasons babies cry:

- Being hungry or tired
- When there is a change in sleep state or body position
- Being over stimulated
- Having to discharge energy
- When they are frustrated, anxious, or fearful
- When there is an upset in routine

Crying needs to be responded to as soon as possible. Babies need to know they have been heard. Crying for long periods serves no purpose to the baby's well being. When you are not able to go to a crying baby immediately, tell the baby that you hear him and you will be coming. This voice response acknowledges that the baby has been heard. This may help him to wait knowing you will be coming to care for him. This may help to reduce the length of time a baby cries. Recognizing what emotional responses you have to a crying baby can help your understanding of when and how you respond to baby's crying. Adults who get anxious when a baby cries may respond too quickly to try to fix the crying rather than to understand why the baby is crying. This often affects the accuracy of the care the baby receives.

It is important to give full uninterrupted attention when caregiving a baby; however sometimes in center care, two or more babies may cry as a way to call you to their need. This may happen when you are already caring for a baby. Rather than fragment your care process by putting down the baby you are caring for, try to:

1. Acknowledge in a soothing voice the baby who is crying by saying, "Jacob, I hear you and I will come as soon as I am done feeding Jamil."
2. Repeat if necessary, trying to soothe the crying baby.
3. See if another caregiver is available to check on Jacob to see what he needs.
4. Go to Jacob as soon as you are available, saying "I know how hard it was for you to wait." Over time, when done repeatedly, Jacob will learn to wait a bit longer because he has learned that he can trust that you will come.

Infants Interacting Together

Rationale:

Infants can engage in meaningful exploration with one another when they have opportunities to do so in a safe environment. They can learn by observing and experiencing each other. Adults can provide opportunities for babies to play and be together by offering a safe play environment with a variety of objects to manipulate.

Goals:

- To understand infants can learn from one another through their exploration and play together
- To let babies be together during play opportunities
- To provide safe spaces for infants to be together

Process:

1. Place two babies near each other in the designated safe play space. Make sure that their physical needs are satisfied beforehand.
2. Provide 2 to 3 objects around the babies within close proximity of their vision and body so each baby can be able to explore and manipulate the objects.

✔ When caregivers allow babies to engage with each other during playtimes, babies learn important interactions that support human relationships.

Gross Motor Movement

Rationale:

Babies are often put into positions they are not yet ready to assume on their own. When this happens, babies are not able to support themselves and be in proper body balance and alignment. Babies who continually are put in positions they cannot support feel helpless and their feeling of helplessness has an effect on their emotional well being.

Goals:

- To support babies natural ability to move
- To allow babies to move in positions they can assume on their own
- To allow babies to move freely without the aid of contraptions

Movement Principles:

- Baby's first position is on their back.
- Babies need to find their own positions in their own time and readiness.
- Avoid placing babies in positions they cannot support on their own.
- Babies roll, turn, and sit up at their own readiness.
- Babies should not be placed in contraptions like swings, highchairs, or bouncy seats.
- Babies need space to move freely.
- Babies need comfortable clothing that does not hamper their movement.
- Babies need to feel secure when they are picked up.
- Babies need their head, neck, and spine supported when being picked up.
- Babies should not be pulled by their arms or legs. This is disrespectful and can injure the child.

Play

Rationale:

Babies play when they are not engaged in a caregiving relationship with an adult caregiver or sleeping. Through play, infants develop their physical, cognitive, language, and social-emotional domains. Play is motivated from within. Play is something that even the youngest infant does when noticing their hands.

When babies play, they learn to choose and grasp objects of interest to them. When we teach play, it becomes our play process instead of the baby's.

The adult role is to set a safe and developmentally appropriate environment, observe for needs, and enjoy baby's play. Sit close by and allow the babies to play without interruption. Knowing when to be available to the baby requires close observation of cues from the baby. When you respond to the baby's cues, you let him know he has been heard.

Goals:

- To allow babies to move freely without the aid of contraptions, i.e. swings, walkers, Johnny Jump Ups, etc.
- To allow babies to choose objects, and explore during their own play process
- To develop and maintain a clean, safe, and developmentally appropriate environment
- To observe babies needs and comfort level

Process:

When the baby is awake and his needs have been met:

1. Prepare the environment before hand for safety and appropriateness.
2. Place the baby in the play environment.
3. Make sure there are two or three varied objects the baby can choose to grasp when ready.
4. Objects need to be chosen depending on baby's ability.
5. Objects need to vary in texture, size, shape, color, and function
6. The caregiver sits nearby, watches, and is available if and when needed.

Outdoor Infant Play

Outdoor play needs to be included as a part of the infant's playtime. Even the very youngest infant can be carried out and placed on their back in a covered canopy area to enjoy the fresh air and what nature offers the infant's senses.

The older infant who can explore on her own should be able to have the option to freely choose when she might want to go outdoors. Creating a space that is fenced in directly outside the infant room is ideal. The space needs to be large enough to accommodate 3-4 infants. It should also be shaded and offer a variety of interesting objects and manipulatives to investigate. A deck leading off the infant room would be a wonderful space to develop for infants to use on their own and in their own time.

Indoor Infant Play

Room Arrangement:

- Safe (from the baby's point of view)
- Simple, clean, orderly
- Developmentally appropriate
- Provide a play space separate from caregiving routines
- Provides indoor and outdoor spaces
- Comfortable (proper heat, ventilation, light, noise control)
- Baby friendly furniture, objects, and adult friendly furniture
- Has enough space for movement, exploration, discovery, choice, and problem solving
- Provide a variety of manipulatives for fine motor exploration and a structure for gross motor development

Play Objects Properties:

- Safe and simple
- Appropriate for stage of baby's development
- Able to be mouthed (tube test)
- Able to be cleaned
- Varied in size, color, shape, weight and texture
- Have different functions
- Requires action of baby to become animated

Adult Response:

- Prepare and maintain the play environment
- Sit nearby and at eye level of the baby
- Observe baby's need and intervene when needed for care routines
- Be available but not interfering
- Place same stage babies near each other for infant-infant interactions
- Let babies choose their play objects and length of play sequence
- Reflect what you see avoiding judgments and/or praise
- Appreciate and enjoy the baby's play

AVOID

- Bright colors
- Loud noise
- Too many people and unnecessary visits
- Improper handling of baby
- Restrictive clothing
- Contraptions such as bouncy seats, exer-saucers, swings, etc.
- Mobiles

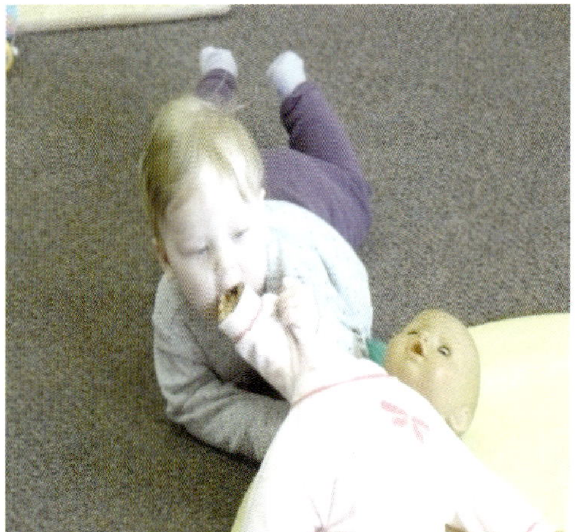
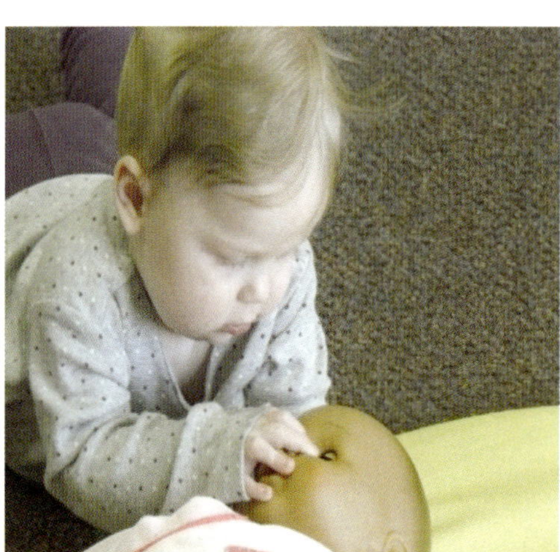

Let babies choose their play objects and length of play sequence

DO

- Use pastels and soft colors
- Use normal tone of voice
- Play soft music 20 minutes, 3 times a day
- Inform visitors of ground rules like washing hands and removing shoes upon entry
- Hold head, neck, and spine securely when picking up and putting down
- Dress baby in comfortable clothes for the weather
- Place babies on their back, allow free movement and exploration

Language

Rationale:

Babies absorb the language of the culture they exist in. They learn to understand language by hearing it, observing verbal and non-verbal cues and responding to the cues. Language is comprehended before it is reproduced. The caregiving relationship is a wonderful opportunity to provide a rich language experience for babies.

Goals:

- To provide an environment rich in verbal and non-verbal language responses
- To speak normal language to the baby when relating to him/her
- To sportscast to the baby what you see
- To let the baby know what you are doing before you do it
- To wait for the baby to respond before continuing your dialogue and include the baby's response in your next interaction

Process of acquiring language:

1. Talk to the baby about what is happening.
2. Use short simple sentences.
3. Tell what you are doing to the baby.
4. Describe the baby's reactions.
5. Acknowledge when the baby is responsive.
6. Sing short songs.
7. Read simple, 2-3 word books to the baby.
8. Name objects for the baby (i.e. ball, doll, bird).

Materials that Aid Language Development:

- Comfortable chair for lap reading
- Pictures at eye level that depict real and familiar objects (i.e. doll, mother, baby, father, bird, ball, etc...)
- Rattles that make it easier for babies to see how the sound is made
- Life like dolls
- Soft cloth books with one object per page
- Books that represent tactile (touch) such as rough/smooth
- CD player for music
- Teacher reference books with songs (i.e. lullabies, finger plays, etc.)
- Manipulatives that offer a variety of shape, color, texture, sound, size, and different functions (i.e. balls, rattles, soft objects, shiny objects, etc.)

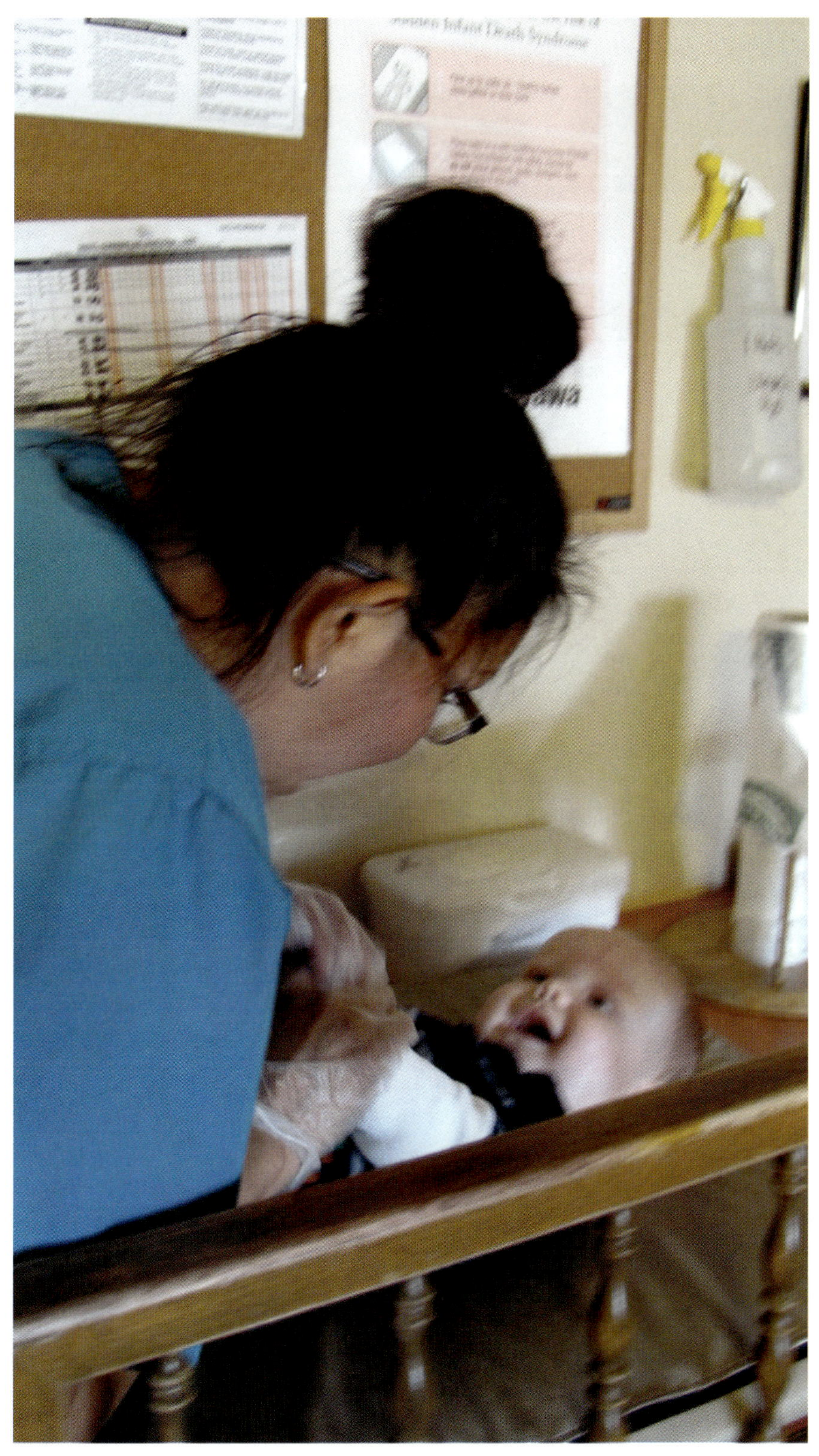

Babies learn to understand language by hearing it, observing cues and responding to the cues. This caregiver is providing an environment that is rich in both verbal and non-verbal language cues by leaning toward the baby, making eye contact, and talking to her about what is happening.

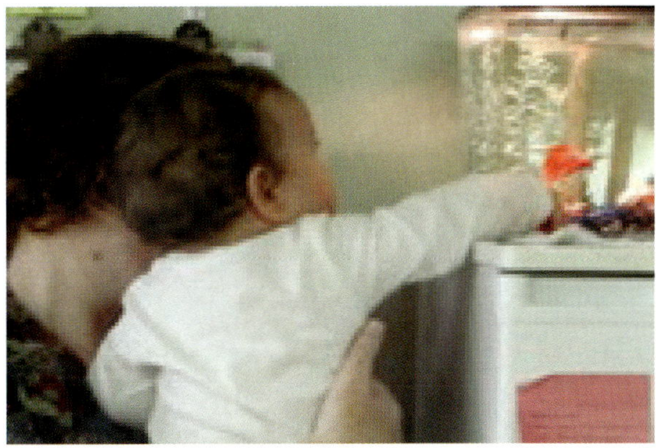

Language Development

0-6 month babies:

- Coo, make raspberries, babble, and may say first intentional word
- Imitate sounds and make utterances
- Respond to their name
- Recognize familiar and different voices
- Respond to facial expressions, like a smile
- Become vocal when spoken to
- Turn toward sounds they hear
- Mouth objects
- Look at objects and pictures
- Prefer contrasting pictures

At 6 months, their listening increases to 600 words.

6-12 month babies:

- Include all of the above and imitate simple sounds
- Respond to simple commands
- May give object or book to adult
- Tear paper and pages
- Laugh, smile, point, and gesture

Literacy Checklist (0-15 months)

Literacy activities are introduced when the child is developmentally ready. Introduction of literacy support activities increases as the infant grows. Literacy support remains part of the infant's environment once introduced.

Age:	Early Literacy Materials
0-8 months	1. Vinyl and cloth books with different textures and sounds. 2. Soothing music; tape recorder, CD player and CDs. 3. Comfortable chairs for lap reading. 4. Soft dolls, pet and farm animal objects. 5. Toys that rattle and make sound. 6. Life like real pictures (i.e., mom, dad, baby, ball, etc.).
9-15 months	1. Books with familiar objects. 2. Board books with easy to turn pages. 3. Theme books with pictures and few words. 4. Simple stories from baby's experiences. 5. Repetitive sing-along interactive songs. 6. Rhyming stories and songs with simple phrases that are repeated. 7. Comfortable chairs for lap reading. 8. Child sized tables and chairs. 9. Pictures and posters of life like objects. 10. Labeled objects and photos. 11. Toys such as stacking blocks, nesting cubes, shape sorters. 12. Objects that encourage pretend play such as a telephone. 13. Stuffed animals and lifelike dolls. 14. Age appropriate puzzles. 15. Art supplies like large crayons, paint, and paper.

Basic Concepts of Group Care

1. Babies need a primary care person who they can rely on to know and care for them.
2. Babies need sensitive responsive care through voice, touch, and eye contact.
3. Babies need to be part of the caregiving process.
4. Babies need to hear the language of the culture they exist in.
5. Babies need care based on their individual body rhythm.
6. Babies need opportunities to participate and cooperate during their care process.
7. Babies need space to freely move, explore, and discover.
8. Babies need adults to observe them before they interact with them.
9. Babies need predictable routines they can trust and rely on.
10. Babies need to be given the process and try to resolve their own struggles rather than be rescued prematurely.
11. Babies need to be with other babies at the same compatible stage.
12. Babies do not need to be entertained and over stimulated during playtime.
13. Babies need opportunities to have peaceful time alone to process information.

Basic Principles for Infant Caregivers

- Primary caregiving with a preferred adult
- Respectful, responsive, reciprocal relationship
- Physically, cognitively, emotionally challenging, and developmentally appropriate safe predictable environment
- Support natural readiness and development
- Freedom to explore on own gross motor ability
- Full presence during caregiving routines
- Participant observer: observe more, do less
- Time for uninterrupted play
- Support same stage infant-infant interactions
- Allow struggle in guided framework
- Use normal language to support comprehension and understanding
- Trust the capability and competence of the infant and toddler for his developmental stages

Large Muscle Observation

Choose one baby to watch their large muscle movements for 5 minutes and answer the questions below afterwards.

1. What parts of the body did you see the baby move? Were the movements smooth and fluid or jerky?

2. Did you see these movements repeated and if so, how many times?

3. What amazed you about the way the baby moved?

4. What did you learn from the baby's movements?

5. What position did the baby move into by his own effort?

6. What position did the baby seem the most comfortable in?

7. In what position did the baby appear most active?

8. How long did the baby stay in one position?

9. In what position did the baby seem most able to concentrate? Was he on his back or stomach?

Hand Movement Observation

Day Schools
Tulsa, Oklahoma

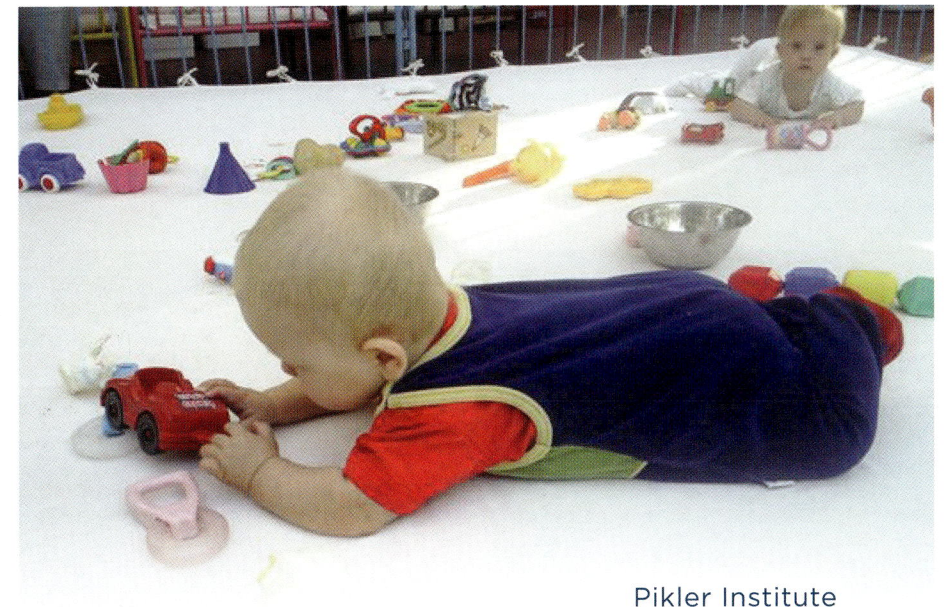

Pikler Institute
Budapest, Hungary

Hand Movement Observation

Choose one baby to watch his hand movements for 5 minutes and answer the questions below afterwards.

1. What did the baby do with his hands?
2. Were the hand movements quick or slow?
3. What did the baby grasp on his own?
4. How many objects did the baby grasp?
5. How long did the baby stay with one object?
6. How often did the baby bring his hand to his mouth?
7. What objects did the baby mouth?
8. What object did the baby seem interested in?
9. Did the baby transfer objects from one hand to the other?

The Toddler Philosophy of Group Care

Toddlers (15-36 months) are unique explorers and scientists who use their whole bodies to experience and investigate the world in which they live.

The curriculum for toddlers is based on several proven learning theories and draws from a variety of approaches. For example, when the adult understands the importance of Erikson's Second stage of psychosocial development for toddlers (autonomy vs. shame) the adult is able to provide opportunities for toddlers to collaborate and participate in their daily living skills (such as helping to dress and undress themselves during the toileting process). The curriculum needs to reflect all toddler developmental domains to challenge the toddler's continued growth, development, and learning.

Because toddlers learn best through their whole body and senses, the adult needs to provide ample opportunities for "hands on" learning activities the toddler can experience. Child size friendly furniture and equipment needs to be accessible to the toddler so that he or she can be an active participant in his/her learning environment. The environment for the toddler needs to assist the toddler to function in ways that provide him with opportunities to demonstrate his budding autonomy and self help skills. The toddler needs to feel "this is my place".

Of particular importance is the ability to support the toddler's growing need for independence. This can be reflected through enhancement of daily life skills such as pouring his own milk, helping to put shoes on, and being part of the toileting process.

The toddler needs easy access to a rich language environment with materials that he is familiar with in his daily life. The adult needs to provide ample opportunities for the toddler to be able to hear spoken words in clear, concise, language as well as identify and label objects in the environment that are of interest to him.

Predictable routines, simple transitions, and safe guidelines help toddlers understand the world in which they relate and help them to have more success in their social encounters with others.

Toddlers also need to have a consistent and nurturing significant adult, have space to move and explore in a safe environment, have choice and problem solving opportunities and be able to have social experiences with peers. The curriculum and environment need to incorporate the standards for best practices for children as recommended by the National Association for the Education for Young Children (NAEYC) as well as your federal, state, and local guidelines.

Goals:

1. To establish a primary relationship with each toddler
2. To respect each toddler as a unique individual with a right to express personal preferences
3. To provide predictable routines during daily experiences
4. To model socio-emotional behaviors that foster respect and empathetic response toward others
5. To foster a growing need for independence in toddlerhood
6. To provide a learning climate that allows each toddler to achieve his/her optimum level of development
7. To provide safe limits and a rich environment that is responsive to all developmental domains
8. To set safe limits for toddlers to exist and relate in their environment with others
9. To allow toddlers uninterrupted time to develop preferences and concentration
10. To assist toddlers in developing self help skills

Toddlers learn best by:

- Having a relationship with a significant adult
- Using their bodies and senses
- Purposeful movement
- Choosing activities
- Repetition
- Activities that relate to their interests
- Experiencing predictability
- Being actively involved in their process

15-36 month Toddler tasks include:

- To participate in daily living skills
- To perfect their movements (large and fine motor) and learn about spatial relationships
- To make choices
- To identify their need and know when to ask for help
- To express feelings
- To think and learn to problem solve
- To have opportunity to exert maximum effort
- To have sensory experiences
- To test reality and limits
- To separate from parents in healthy ways
- To develop awareness of others
- To gain self help and self regulation skills

Toddler Characteristics:

- Scientists and explorers
- In a push-pull struggle between dependency and independency
- Egocentric (me, mine)
- Into power
- Test limits
- Enjoy cause and effect experiences
- Raw emotion
- Little concept of spatial relationships
- Learning coordination
- Very concrete
- Gain trust from predictable order
- May have limited language expression
- Learn by doing and hands on experiences
- Ignite and explode (temper tantrum) easily
- Thrive on repetition

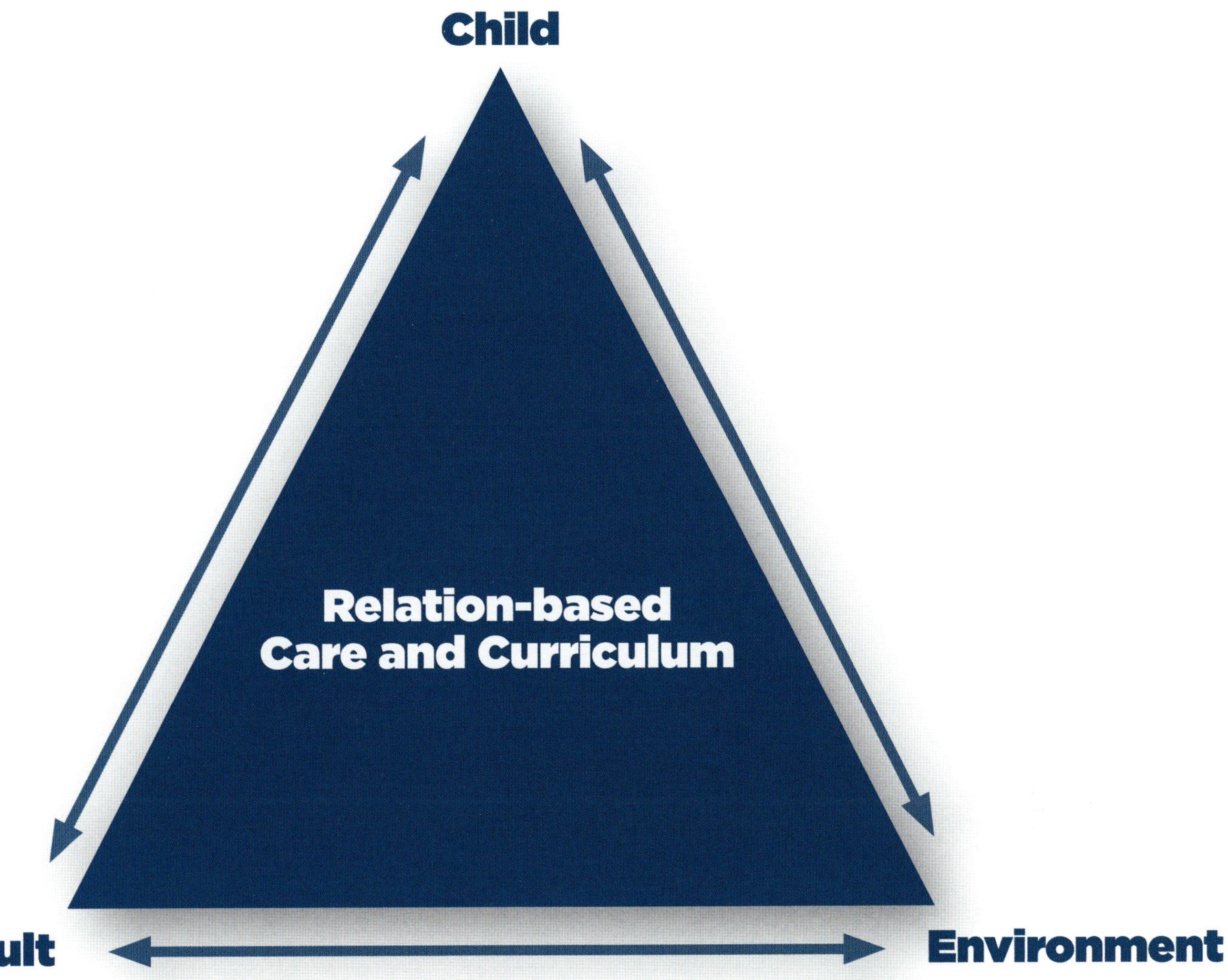

This diagram represents the dynamic and interdependent relationship between the child, the environment and the adult. The learning environment needs to reflect the developmental needs of the toddler while allowing the toddler to participate for his level of function. The adult relates to the environment by keeping the environment in a constant state of readiness. The adult is available as a model and guide to assist the toddler when needed. The toddler learns he can rely on the adult when he needs assistance and cooperates with the adult in the care of his body. The toddler learns to relate to the environment as an opportunity to develop his skill, autonomy, and competence.

Day
Schools

Basic Concepts of Group Care

Toddlers need:

1. Involvement with a consistent primary caregiver. A caregiver who is sensitive and responsive to the toddlers in his or her care.
2. To be acted with, not upon. Their participation is vital to their understanding during the caregiving process.
3. Their individual cues and signals to be understood and responded to by a caring adult.
4. To hear language of the culture they live in.
5. Individualized care based on their body's need and function rather than a room schedule.
6. Opportunities to participate and cooperate in their caregiving routines.
7. Time to explore, discover, and move freely in their environment.
8. Predictable, clear routines based on sequence of events.
9. Opportunities to problem solve their own struggles rather than be rescued prematurely.
10. To be able to interact and socialize with other toddlers.
11. Time to process information and cues during transitions from one activity to another.

Caregiver Behaviors that Support the Toddler Curriculum

Caregivers need to:

1. Support the need for toddlers to move freely and offer them choice in activities.
2. Set clear, simple, and safe limits.
3. Understand that the toddler's "no" is the beginning of autonomy.
4. Offer choice into the toddler's day.
5. Provide opportunities for toddlers to be helpful when caring for themselves and their environment.
6. Incorporate sand or water into the toddlers' daily activities.
7. Develop a curriculum that is rich in sensory activities.

Caregiver Behaviors that Support the Toddler Curriculum

8. Frame language in positive ways that promote the behavior they want to happen (i.e., "feet on floor" instead of "get down off the table").
9. Have cause and effect represented in the environment (i.e., toddlers like to bang and clang objects).
10. Help toddlers express their emotions as well as give simple explanations relating to limitations, ie. "I know it was hard for you to wait"
11. Express language in specific and clear ways with proper labels given to objects.
12. Assist toddlers in learning about spatial relationships through delineating space in the environment.
13. Provide ample opportunities for toddlers to master self help, learn to self regulate, and build self sufficiency and confidence.
14. Set up environments based on the toddlers' ability and readiness.
15. Provide gross motor structures in the environment for toddlers to use their large muscles.
16. Provide environments that allow toddlers to develop concentration through play and curricular activities.

Incorporate sand or water into the toddlers' daily activities.

Use furniture and rugs to delineate space in the environment

Provide well defined areas to allow toddlers to develop concentration through play.

The Art of Observation

Definition:

Observation is an art and skill, which you can use to learn, appreciate, and understand the toddler. It is a way of assessing how the toddler is doing in relation to himself, others, and the environment.

Getting ready to observe:

- Observe daily for at least five minutes.
- Sit in one place.
- Quiet yourself to become peaceful.
- Empty your head of thoughts.
- Pick one toddler, a peer interaction, or toddlers relating in their environment.
- Stay focused in the here and now.
- Watch, look, and see.

Benefits of the observation:
By observing more:

- You appreciate each individual toddler's unique way of relating.
- You begin to learn what the toddler can do and is not yet ready to do.
- You learn that each toddler has his or her own signals or cues that tell you something.
- You allow toddlers to help you to understand them.
- You learn to appreciate and enjoy the pleasure of just being with toddlers.
- You gain understanding of how toddlers relate to others and to their environment.
- You assess and assist in problem solving situations.

Toddler Observation

Pick one toddler to observe in one or more of these categories.

I. Movement Indoors – body and spatial awareness–

a. Describe his body movements (jerky, smooth, balanced, etc.)

b. Is judgment and balance a part of the way the toddler moves?

c. Is he safe during movement?

d. Is the toddler aware of the furniture, objects, and space around him as he moves through the environment?

e. Can he hold an object in his hands while walking?

f. Is he able to successfully navigate through the room and the pathways provided in the environment?

g. Is he aware of his peers as he moves through space?

II. Movement outdoors – large motor activities:

a. What kind of gross motor movements did you notice the toddler doing (jumping, climbing, etc.)?

b. What kind of outdoor activities was he involved with (trikes, balls, etc.)?

c. Did he play with any other children? What peer interactions did you notice?

III. Fine motor activities – activity

a. Is the toddler able to choose an object or activity of interest?

b. Can he concentrate on one activity at a time? For how long?

c. How is he able to use his hands?

d. Is he able to transfer objects from one hand to the other?

e. How does he play with manipulatives (build, strings, blocks, etc...?)

f. What does he do to show he is able to participate in his care (i.e. dress and undress, put on shoes, etc?)

Observe the group

IV. Play and Interactions

a. Were the children playing with each other?
b. What type of play activities were the children involved in?
c. Were the children allowed to play uninterrupted?
d. Were the children able to choose their objects of play?
e. Did you notice any children developing friendships between one another?
f. Was there any struggle or conflicts around objects between children? How was this handled?
g. Describe the play environment and atmosphere.
h. Describe the attitude of the adult during play activities.
i. What kind of adult interactions did you notice with the children?
j. Did you notice any child withdrawing from the play activities? What was done?
k. How were acts of aggression handled?
l. How were children acknowledged or treated with respect?

V. Social - Emotional

a. Did you notice crying? How was it handled?
b. Did the children understand what to expect from adults? Were the routines predictable and a part of signaling the toddler for change?
c. Did the children use language to express their needs?
d. Did the children ask for help or assistance when needed?
e. Did the children listen for a short period of time (i.e. story)?
f. Explain how transitions were handled (i.e., safe, chaotic)
g. Were the children able to participate in their caregiving routines? Describe.
h. Were the children able to solve simple problems?
i. Did you notice any self-soothing behaviors from children? Explain.

Day School

Cooperative Toileting

Rationale:

Toileting occurs as a one on one experience between you and the toddler. Toileting is a very personal experience that requires the full attention and cooperation of the toddler and caregiver. It requires an experience that is sensitive, responsive, and rich in a dialogue between the caregiver and the toddler. The communication needs to reflect what is happening in the present here and now. Language about what is taking place is important to understand each other's valuable gestures and cues. As the toddler experiences the caregiver's attention to his behavior, he will understand what is expected and will also feel acknowledged. When this occurs, the toddler is more likely to cooperate and participate during the caregiving process. As you slow down, you interpret important signals and cues from the toddler that enable you to respond accurately. Slowing down helps you to understand what is taking place and allows the toddler time to process information. Interruptions interfere with the quality of the toileting process and should be avoided.

Goals:

- To be fully aware and involved during one on one toileting between the caregiver and the toddler
- To toilet in a bathroom away from high traffic areas in a calm peaceful environment that is equipped with necessary items for toilet success
- To dialogue about what is happening between you and the toddler
- To observe and respond to important gestures and cues from the toddler
- To allow the toddler time to participate and cooperate for his stage of development

Process:

1. Check bathroom beforehand for available items for successful and sanitary toileting.
2. Wash your hands and go to the toddler, telling him that it is time to use the toilet.
3. Toddlers can walk to the bathroom by themselves or can hold the caregiver's hand. Offer your hand to the toddler to see if he will take it.
4. Toddlers can stand while diapering.
5. Put gloves on, letting the toddler see and feel the different texture of skin and glove.
6. A child sized chair for the child and one for the adult needs to be available for assisting during dressing and undressing.
7. Verbally describe the clothes you are helping to remove and ask for the toddler to help. Slowly take off any clothing with the help of the toddler (i.e. taking down his

pants, removing the diaper, etc.). Give the toddler time to help and interpret what you are saying.

8. Offer the toddler opportunities to assist as much as he is able during the care process (i.e. "Can you help by lifting your shirt?" or "I see you can lift your shirt by yourself."). Some toddlers have more self help skills than others. Observing during the toileting process will help you understand each toddler's level of ability.
9. Clean the child's private area with an unscented wipe or preferably a moist paper towel.
10. Allow the child to discard the bagged soiled diaper in a pedal trash can. Refrain from using the word "dirty" to describe the diaper. Instead say "soiled" or other word that is less negative.
11. Take off your gloves.
12. Invite the child to sit on the toilet.
13. Have sturdy wooden stairs with rails to help the child get up to the toilet.
14. Have your hands available as a guide if needed.
15. Tell the child to give his body a "chance" if he looks impatient or in a hurry to get off the toilet seat. Sometimes hearing running water helps children who are having difficulty. Your attitude should convey that using the bathroom is a normal bodily function.
16. When the child initiates readiness to get off the toilet, be available to guide with your hands if needed.
17. Let the child flush the toilet and watch the water go down and back into the bowl. See his reaction and comment on what you can see happening.
18. Allow the toddler to get his fresh diaper or training pants.
19. Allow him to assist in dressing himself as much as he is able. He may need to sit in a chair or stool for part of the dressing.
20. Have a dialogue about what is happening while making eye contact during the toileting process.
21. When the child is ready, let him wash and dry his hands at the sink with running water.
22. Be sure to wash your hands.
23. Remember to:
    - Say what you are going to do.
    - Observe.
    - Wait for the toddler to process and respond.
    - Tell the toddler what you see him doing.
    - Reflect your observation and actions to the toddler.

Toilet Environment:

- In a bathroom, away from high traffic areas, and near a water source
- Toileting items need to be accessible to the child
- Lidded pedal diaper container
- Gloves, plastic bags, wipes, and paper towels
- Personal items (diapers, change of clothes)
- Running water source

Note:

1. Be available and fully present with the toddler.
2. Maintain predictable diapering/ toileting routines.
3. Allow toddler participation and cooperation.
4. Remain patient, consistent, and informative.
5. Follow all sanitary toileting procedures.
6. Record information.

Toilet Learning

In center-based care, toilet training is a process that begins in the infant room by creating an atmosphere of peaceful quality time. The child is encouraged to be a cooperative member of the diapering process. The movement from the diaper changing table (a lift up) to a standing position in the bathroom usually takes place when the child gives us "cues" as to his or her own readiness. One beginning sign is that the toddler is aware of being soiled and wants the diaper taken off.

Usually the child responds to this "milestone" by watching other children use the bathroom. The adult role is one of matter of fact acceptance and support to the child during this natural process. Never force a child, get into a power struggle with a child, or verbally reprimand a child over toileting. Reward and or punishment has no place in the toileting process. When a child has an accident, it's expected at this age, accept this as a natural occurrence and utilize the accident as a learning opportunity.

By the time the child is two, the approach should be even more collaborative and independent between the carer and the child. The child is changed standing up and all items for the toileting are close at hand. This allows for the child to assist in his/her bathroom care. Each child is offered to sit on the toilet and the caregiver uses normal language to describe what is happening (i.e. toilet, urine, etc.). There is a small chair and an adult chair for dressing and undressing during the toilet process of the toddler.

Clothing should be simple for the child to take off and put on. As caregivers or parents working with children on toilet learning, encourage the child to take charge of his body and help him to become more competent in his ability to help himself. In this way, home and school can be working together to provide consistent toilet training.

Who is ready for toilet training? Here are signs to look for:

1. A dry diaper – nighttime bladder and bowel control.
2. Dry diaper during the daytime – it is obvious the child's bladder control is to the point where he or she can retain urine for a period of time (about two hours).
3. Bowel movements are somewhat regular in terms of same time of day.
4. The bowel movements are formed and have definite shape.
5. The child may tell you, "I have to pee pee", when in fact he or she has already urinated.
6. The child may ask to use the toilet.
7. The child may tell you he or she needs a change of diaper.
8. The child may anticipate urinating or defecating, then go ahead and do it, showing a genuine awareness.
9. Balance – is the child physically able to sit on the toilet: can he or she get on the toilet independently of the parent?

10. Undressing – is the child capable of pulling down pants and pulling them back up again?

How to approach a child for toilet learning

When you feel the child is ready and have noticed many of the signs, you can begin with toilet learning. Your approach is critically important to the outcome of toilet learning. This is a natural process. Toileting is something we do every day of our lives. There is nothing to be ashamed of or inhibited about. It is important to be relaxed and very positive. Before the child actually sits on the toilet, it is a good idea to begin to prepare the child or ease the child carefully into the idea of using the toilet (i.e., let him flush the toilet to let him see the water go down and then back into the toilet bowl). Don't force the child on the toilet. Allow the child to watch other family members use the toilet. He or she will get an accurate idea of what is expected.

It is helpful to read a book about using the toilet. An exceptionally good one is *Toilet Learning: The Picture Book Technique for Children and Parents,* by Allison Mach (Little, Brown and Company, 1978).

It is also a good idea to introduce pants with an elastic waistband. Show the child how to pull them down and then how to pull the pants up. Introduce underpants, not necessarily trying them on unless the child wants to.

Using the toilet

It is important to establish a routine schedule. Encourage the child to use the toilet every morning when he or she gets up, after all meals, maybe once or twice during the morning, before nap time, after nap time, etc. You will have to decide the best routine for your child by observing his own preferences. As a primary caregiver, you know how much your child consumes and how often he or she needs to eliminate.

There should be a predictable routine every time the child does use the toilet. Encourage the child to take care of himself. He or she needs to pull down pants, place himself on the toilet, if able, wipe himself, pull up his pants, flush, and then wash his hands.

Just a note on flushing: if the child resists, just flush the toilet yourself. For some children, flushing away their feces is more than they can bear, they consider it a part of themselves or are afraid of the water leaving the toilet bowl.

A note on hand washing: for some unknown wonderful reason, children this age love water. When the child gets to the sink to wash his hands, please do not lose all your patience and understanding at this step of the toilet training. What's a little spilled water? The child probably will enjoy mopping it up with a towel. Remember, stay relaxed and positive.

If the child is catching on, bring out the underpants. If the child is wearing underpants, then he has complete independence in using the toilet. He does not have to deal with pulling off the diaper. Remember, when it is time for underpants and no more diapers, be gentle and positive. Once you introduce underpants it is not a good idea to also use diapers, this can be confusing to the child. So, be sure the child and you are ready for underpants and expect accidents to happen.

About accidents

Expect them frequently in the beginning. There will be many in the first week of toilet learning. Do not scold, spank, or punish the child in any way. Above all, you do not want your child to have negative feelings about using the toilet. Remember, this is very new to your child and it does take some time to learn.

If the child is truly ready to learn to use the toilet, by the second week the accidents will be far less frequent. The third week there will be even less and probably none. By week four, if the child is still having accidents, this indicates that he is not ready.

Regressions

In the initial learning period, there may seem to be regression in the child. There can be many causes. Among these are the parent out of town, a new sitter, relocating, or the birth of a sibling. Anything upsetting to the child or out of the child's normal routine can cause regression. Usually this regression state does not last long if the child is truly ready for toilet learning. Try not to introduce toileting when there are major transitions in the child's family life. Toileting itself is a major transition for the child.

Remember that toilet learning before a child is ready can inhibit the child's development in other areas. It can cause the child to feel somewhat stressed. Some children deal with stress unconsciously. Some examples are stuttering, physical aggression, constipation, continued pants wetting (accidents) or a nervous bladder.

When caregivers force a child to practice the steps to toileting, it is unnecessary and stressful for the child. Magda Gerber likened this repetitive practice of the toileting process to a nightmare image of a miniature Charlie Chaplin moving quickly and repeatedly through the steps of going to the potty while the parent looks on, coaching each step and urging them to do it quickly.

Magda replied, "I cannot help having a frantic nightmare at this point. I see miniature Charlie Chaplins moving quickly to the potty chair, urinating, eating salted crackers, drinking more fluid, standing up, pulling pants up, down quickly, quickly, faster, faster, stop. It seems like the caricature of a future shock world for children". The reality is that once a child decides to use the toilet, he knows how to do it. It is unnecessary to teach, practice, exercise the little techniques. Children do learn to dress and undress themselves if parents encourage cooperation every time they care for them. If each diapering has been a pleasurable experience, a true dialogue between parent and child, if the caregiver has given her full attention during all these times, there will be no need for the special circus performance.

Toilet learning happens as a result of

a healthy, normal child, living in an average accepting, caring family. As part of his natural development, the child wants to be like and act like his parents. The child has to be ready physically (capacity of the bladder to hold more fluid, better muscle control), cognitively (be fully aware of what he is expected to do), and emotionally (be ready and willing to give up a comfortable situation, such as just letting urine and feces out whenever it does so naturally). For the child, it means that he has to delay and control a natural urge, to give away something he may believe is still part of his body, and therefore valuable, and to conform to an adult-designed routine. It is an area and a time of inner conflict. "But, like the prince of the fairy tale, he, the child, fights his battles and masters the difficulties to gain the love and admiration of his first idol - his parent"(Magda Gerber, 1979).

Though these are lifelong struggles, they seem to be crucial during the anal stage of development. Erikson writes, "This (anal) stage therefore becomes decisive for the ratio of love and hate, cooperation and willfulness, freedom of self-expression and its suppression. From a sense of self-control without loss of self-esteem comes a lasting sense of good will and pride; from a sense of loss of self control and of foreign over-control comes a lasting propensity for doubt and shame." Rushing the young child through toileting may cause later developmental delays.

Routines that Decrease Chaos

Routines that Decrease Chaos

Rationale:

Routines are considered a part of the curriculum for toddlers and are an essential part of the toddler and adult relationship. It is through routines that adults and toddlers interact in mutual and satisfying ways. It is the adult's responsibility to provide safe clear routines that help toddlers understand what is happening

Routines need to be carried out:

1. Consistently
2. Predictably
3. Pleasurably and enjoyably
4. Based on the toddler's need
5. Rich in dialogue
6. In ways that include the toddler in the process
7. Incorporating meaningful cues for the toddler
8. Giving the toddler enough time

Goals:

1. To provide a safe and consistent predictable sequence of events the toddler understands and learns to know
2. To provide a collaborative relationship with the toddler rich in language, cues, and responses
3. To provide opportunities for the toddler to cooperate and participate for his level of development

Process:

Gaining insight and knowledge into each individual toddler assists the caregiver to understand the toddler's behavior and preferences. By taking time to diaper, feed, nap, or dress a toddler, you can respond and incorporate their behavior in your process together. When you include the toddlers' cues and responses in caregiving routines, you let him/her know you understand his/her needs and that s/he is valued. Providing predictable routines helps the toddler learn to participate, trust, and enjoy the experience. This fuels a trusting relationship between you and the toddler.

Note:

During caregiving routines, the toddler may lose focus and concentration about what is occurring. When the toddler shows signs of distraction or inattentiveness, the caregiver needs to re-offer and invite the toddler to return to the relationship. This may require you to wait for the toddler to focus back to you. This can be done by saying "look at me" or "I need you to help me". These requests invite the child to return to the caregiving relationship. It also reaffirms to the toddler that you need his valuable participation to be successful in the care routines.

See How We Eat

Rationale:

Toddlers are in group care several hours during a given day. They need frequent nourishment (every 3-4 hours) to maintain energy for their bodies and avoid meltdowns or unnecessary emotional distress.

Many factors influence eating:

- Familial and cultural influences
- Eating preferences and patterns
- Distractions
- How toddlers manage eating skills
- Ability of toddler to be in a group eating situation
- The attitude of the adult and climate of the eating environment

Caregivers need to understand how these factors influence the child's nutritional habits and eating success. Caregivers need to be observant and sensitive to toddler's needs during eating times.

Predictable eating routines allow toddlers to understand what is expected. Caregivers can minimize distractions and provide a peaceful and enjoyable experience for toddlers. Child sized furniture and equipment help the toddler to develop self help skills fostering independence. Setting clear defined limits and expectations, around safety and respect between toddlers is essential during their food experience (i.e. sit while eating). The caregiver observes and is available when needed to ensure the toddlers' ability and participation for his/her stage of development.

Goals:

- To design an appropriate eating area that encourages self-help and self-regulation
- To prepare the eating area for the child to function independently for his level of development
- To support the toddler's need for independence
- To allow each toddler to be actively involved during their eating experience
- To allow each toddler to eat and drink according to his individual body need
- To develop a quiet eating place away from high traffic areas and near a water source
- To establish and maintain clear ground rules for eating that assist toddlers to define limits of acceptable behaviors (i.e. wash hands before eating, eat only from your plate)
- To utilize the eating experience as a learning environment for good nutrition and appropriate habits
- To assist toddlers in developing necessary skills for successful eating

Basic principles on eating:

- Eating is for nourishment.
- Eating is pleasurable and a sensory experience.
- Allow toddlers to eat as much as he needs; the amount should be regulated by the child's needs.
- The eating process is based on the readiness and capability of the child.
- The adult encourages and promotes independence and competency with toddlers.
- Toddlers need to sit at the same designated space while eating or drinking.
- Allow toddlers to participate as much as they are able.
- The process of eating encourages self-regulation, self-initiation, self-help, self-reliance, and self-satisfaction.
- Adults promote respect for one another during eating (avoid bribes, praises, or punishments).

Note:

Children who join the program late in the year may not have had a chance to practice the type of eating experience you offer in the classroom. They may need assistance from the teacher or another peer. This may also be true at the beginning of the year when toddlers have not developed knowledge of the routine or skills necessary for success during mealtimes. Simplify the eating environment for the toddler to function and grow skills. The caregiver is an active role model who demonstrates and explains how to do things. The ground rules are simple, clear, and consistent. When toddlers know what to expect, they will be more likely to understand what to do. This helps children cooperate.

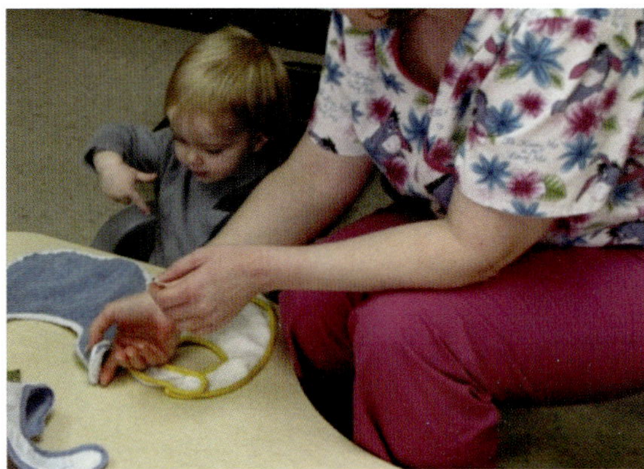

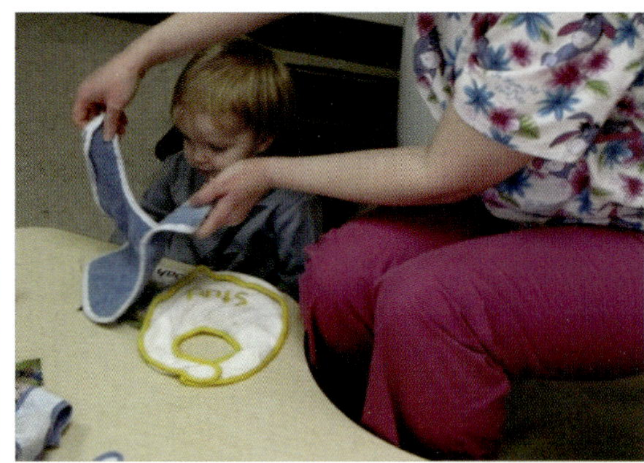

Process for community lunch:

1. Prepare each food item in a bowl and place on table. Allow two children to help set the table with plates, utensils, glasses, napkins, etc.
2. Ask children to wash their hands at the sink.
3. Develop a transition to lunch (i.e., calling each child's name and telling him to sit in his designated space.
4. Help put on bib (if bib is required).
5. Eat with the children as a way to model.
6. Sit with the same group of children in your place. (Have a separate table for extra food items, utensils, drink, sponges, etc.)
7. Pass each bowl of food family style with spoon for self-serving.
8. Label and discuss each food item during lunch ("this is broccoli, broccoli is green...").
9. Place one serving spoon of food on the plate. Avoid overfilling the plate so the toddler does not feel overwhelmed.
10. Let the child eat whatever food he chooses first. Make no distinction between vegetables, meats, carbs, or dessert. For the older toddler, when serving family style allow the toddler to serve himself by using the spoon and/or passing the serving bowls to his peers (when ready).
11. Offer a small amount of liquid in a glass. Offer water first as a way to open the digestive tract.
12. Assist them in pouring liquids if necessary.
13. When the child is done, help him take his bib off, ask him to scrape his plate in the trash and place it and the glass in the bin of dirty dishes. Ask him to wash his hands. Have a transitional activity for children to engage in as this process requires time. (i.e., books to look at, Lego's or other objects to build, etc).
14. One teacher remains sitting with the children while the other monitors the transition activity.

Suggestions for Toddler snacks

- Fresh seasonal fruit (i.e. bananas, apples, etc.)
- Cereal (non-sugar) with low fat or 2% milk
- Applesauce and graham crackers
- Hard boiled eggs and pita bread
- Turkey roll-ups
- Cheese and crackers
- Yogurt with fruit
- Zucchini muffins

Road to Restful Sleep

Rationale:

Helping toddlers to sleep in group care is difficult. Predictable routines, the attitude of the caregiver, and the sleep environment contribute to forming good sleep habits. It is essential for toddlers to develop good sleep habits while at the center.

Toddlers have already developed a pattern for their sleep from their parents. It is a good idea to know how parents put their children to sleep to gain valuable information that assists you in normalizing the toddler's sleep at the center.

Important reference information:

1. Does the toddler take a nap during the day?
2. How long does the toddler nap at home?
3. What time does he go to bed at night?
4. Does he sleep throughout the night?
5. How long does he sleep?
6. Where does he sleep?
7. How is he put to sleep (the process)?
8. Does he have a special love object?
9. Does he need a blanket or pillow?

The sleep space is different from their home. In the center, toddlers have to adjust to many noises, different people coming in and out, different space, and being with other toddlers and adults. Toddlers have to learn to adjust to all these changes in order to be calm enough to fall asleep.

Goals:

- To help toddlers understand and recognize signs of tiredness in their own bodies
- To include and involve toddlers in the process of nap ("Can you turn off the light?", "Please get your blanket", "It's time to put your shoes in your cubby")
- To maintain the same consistent routines
- To provide a sequence of events that leads to easy nap transitions (i.e., decrease in activity and noise level, children getting personal nap items, taking off shoes, reading "Goodnight Moon", etc.)

The care process:

1. Observe signs of tiredness. Reflect what you see happening to his body, "I see you are rubbing your eyes", etc.
2. Allow ample time for toddlers to process during nap transitions (20-30 minutes).
3. Let the toddler help through transitions for rest. (Care of self, get their own bedding, take their shoes off, and pull down shade.)
4. Decrease activity level by providing a calm atmosphere. Read the same short story as part of the nap transition (i.e. Goodnight Moon).
5. Tell the toddler it is time to "rest" his body (avoid using the word "sleep"). Calm your own body down as a model to the toddler.
6. If a child shows resistance and does not want to go to sleep, help him refocus and be part of the process by saying "It is time to rest" reference by saying "I'm tired also and am going to rest next to you." You may have to stay a few extra minutes with a child who is having difficulty calming himself for rest.

Note:

The adult's attitude plays an important role when napping toddlers. Convey a feeling that rest is a natural need of the body. Being clear and matter of fact about rest time helps children accept what is happening. Avoid using extra props like back rubbing, dark rooms, bribes, etc.

Toddlers exhibit self-soothing behavior like:

- Begins to suck fingers or fist
- Yawns
- Rubs eyes
- Quiets self
- Becomes inactive
- Tired or red eyes
- Restlessness or irritability
- Less focus
- Looses balance and falls or bumps into objects.
- Cranky, irritable mood
- Has meltdown

It is important for toddlers to learn to fall asleep on their own biologic rhythm. Less intervention allows the toddler a chance to learn to self-regulate. Self-regulation is a key strength that supports positive mental health.

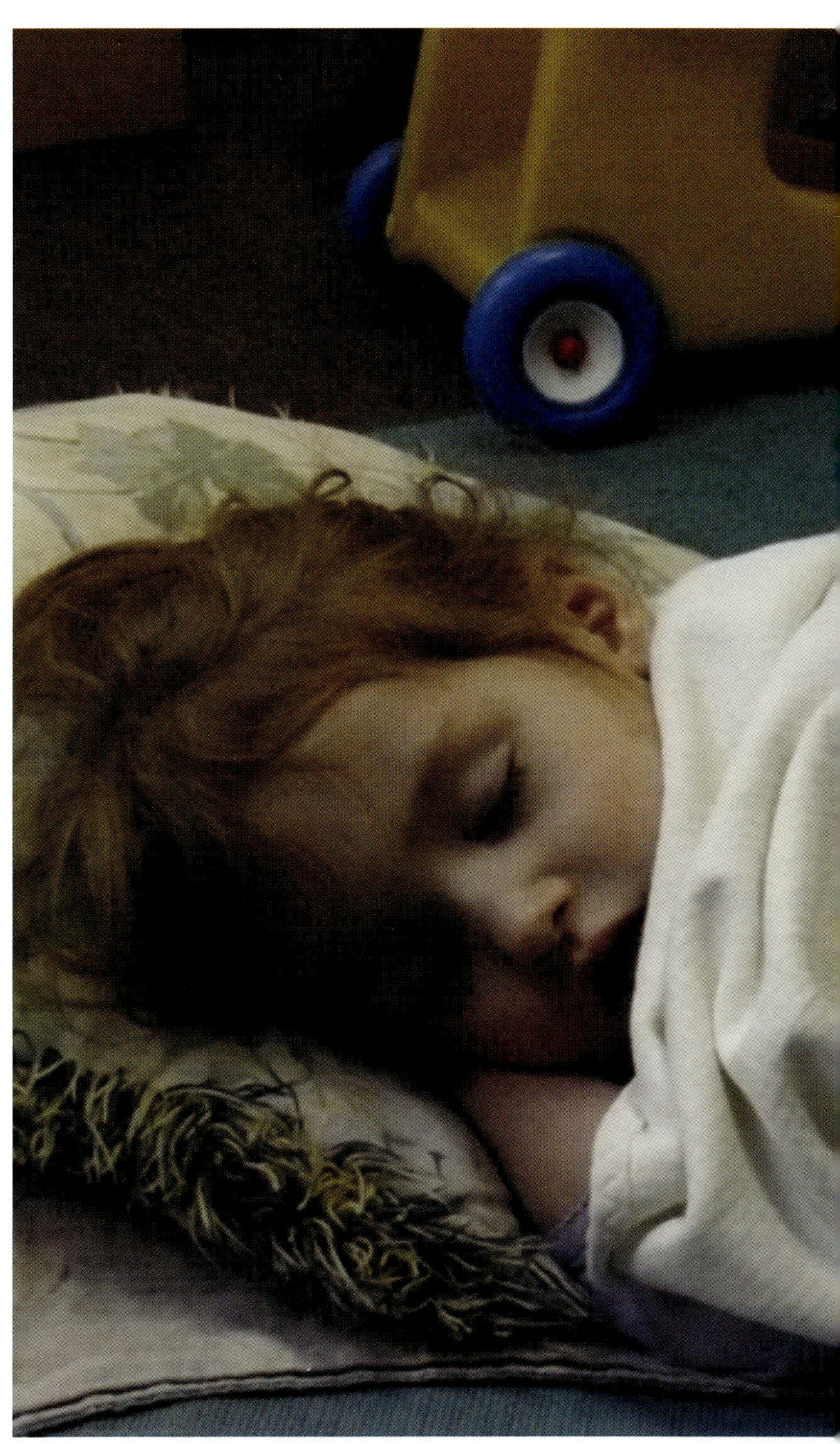

Adult attitude:

Model a matter of fact attitude that the body needs rest:

- Begin to provide a calm and peaceful room environment.
- Develop predictable sleep routines and consistent transitions.
- Use a soft tone of voice and calm, slow body movements.
- Allow the toddler to help during his nap routine. (i.e., take off shoes, get his blanket, etc.).
- Decrease stimulation (i.e. dim the lights). Move from active to quiet behaviors.
- Talk to the child in normal language stating that it is time for rest. You may have to repeat or guide the child to his individual cot. You can offer your hand.
- Portray an attitude that you value rest and how lucky they are to have an opportunity to be kind to their bodies.
- Develop a special behavior that signals the end of the transition and share with each child (i.e. bend down and straighten their blanket as you say "goodnight" with a smile).

Lifesaver Transitions

Rationale:

Transitions are predictable rituals that toddlers learn to trust and rely on. Many toddlers have difficulty during transitions due to their internal emotional struggle between dependency and interdependency. This may interfere with providing calm transitions. This unbalance between dependency and interdependency can cause transitions to be chaotic and unsafe unless there is prior planning.

Maintaining predictability while offering flexibility is an art to toddler curriculum. The caregiver needs to have a large skill base for developing consistent steps leading to successful transitions. Toddlers need to know what those steps are in order to cooperate. Toddlers are at a developmental stage where they test limits and challenge authority in order to gain a sense of what it is that they can and cannot do. It is their way of developing their sense of self. It is a critical time for the toddler to feel safe physically and emotionally. Safety needs to be reflected in terms of clear and predictable patterns that can help the toddler understand what is expected from him.

When the child has a clear understanding of what is going to happen next, he is more likely to participate, and to cooperate. Transitions establish a deep sense of security and promote self-regulation and self-help skills. You are necessary and valuable to insuring transitions are established in safe, clear and supportive ways for the toddler.

Goals:

1. To provide predictable routines based on a sequence of events rather than time
2. To establish routines that are safe, simple, and consistent
3. To maintain safety during transitions
4. To provide clear basic expectations
5. To provide signals that help toddlers understand what is happening
6. To provide enough time, space and movement for the toddler
7. To create activities during transitions that toddlers can participate in and enjoy
8. To create small steps in transitions that minimize confusion and chaos
9. To have clear expectations of the child's abilities

Principles:

- Transitions help decrease chaos and increase safety.
- Transitions help toddlers move from one activity to another with minimal chaos.
- Transitions help connect toddlers socially and emotionally with other toddlers.
- Transitions need to be thought out and planned as part of the toddler's curriculum.
- Transitions help toddlers safely move from one activity to another (i.e. moving from outdoors to indoors).

Process:

- Use a signal to specify transition time (ring bell, turn off light, sing song, etc.).
- Tell the toddlers what you are about to do.
- Allow time for toddlers to act and process (toddlers take more time than adults to process information).
- Give one clear rule or limit or action (i.e. Johnny may go get his coat on.").
- Avoid herding or gathering toddlers.
- Be an active participant in the process of toddler transitions. If one adult is engaged with the group the other should position herself where the children need to go (i.e. caregiver by the door to assist with putting on coats for outdoor play).
- Insure safe transitioning from one activity or environment to another (i.e. moving from outdoor play to indoors for lunch).

Examples of transition to nap:

- Transition from lunch to clean up by allowing one toddler at a time to put dishes in a bin or sink.
- Allow time for individual personal care (diapering, brushing teeth, etc.).
- Develop a story time.
- Prepare for rest (placing cots, personal items, shoes off, etc.).
- Turn out the light.
- Check with each individual child (i.e. cover them with a blanket and say "have a good rest").

Example of transition to outdoors:

- Sing a song or do an interactive fingerplay (i.e. welcome song).
- Assist toddler to dress for outdoors (i.e., put on coat or sweater by calling child's name to go to other caregiver for putting on coat).
- Let child help put on coat (older toddlers may try to help each other).
- Wait at door with one adult.

See How We Play

What Is Play?

Play is what a child does. It is an important part of the development of learning. "Real" play is the process by which a child interacts in his/her environment in such a way that is spontaneous and free. Play is inner-directed and non-goal oriented. Play should never be corrected. It is a child's choice that is respected and should not be interrupted without an apology. Play provides a natural outlet for a child's curiosity, anxiety, and social experiences. Play services a need for a child's mastery. It is the opportunity by which a child works out his/her life's "struggles" and learns how to fit into society. In play, there is no contest. No right or wrong- no win or lose. Play exists for play's sake.

Play

Rationale:

Toddlers learn through play. Toddlers learn about how things work, how to interact with objects and how to relate with others. Through play, toddlers also learn how to problem solve in situations and events. Play can occur for long periods of time if uninterrupted. Toddlers play with objects and toys alone or with others. Play is motivated from within each toddler through his own discovery, experimentation, and exploration. Play does not have to be taught, it happens spontaneously.

The adult's primary role in play is to design and maintain a safe and developmentally appropriate environment that has interesting and varied objects and activities for toddlers to learn, manipulate, and explore. During toddler free play, monitoring the classroom for safety requires concentration and observation on the part of the adult. Active involvement in the toddler's play depends on the toddler's request for you to enter into his play activity.

Pikler Institute
Budapest, Hungary

Goals:

- To allow toddlers to experiment, explore, and discover their own play process
- To allow ample time for uninterrupted free play
- To allow the toddler to choose his objects and activities of play
- To develop and maintain a clean, safe, and developmentally appropriate play space that is in readiness for the toddler
- To sensitively observe the toddler at play in order to evaluate for need and comfort
- To assist the toddler when invited or asked
- To refrain from interrupting the toddler's concentration during play

Process:

1. Observe and prepare the play environment. Be sure all object pieces are complete and in a designated place. A place for everything and everything in its place.
2. Assure that the play environment is in readiness for the toddler to engage in play (no missing pieces, activity in proper place, variety of interesting play objects).
3. Provide a variety of developmentally appropriate objects that vary in size, shape, color, weight, texture, and function.
4. Allow toddlers to choose play objects.
5. Provide uninterrupted free time.
6. Remind toddlers to place objects back in their designated place before selecting other objects.
7. Monitor clear, safe rules around respect of others and equipment.
8. Be emotionally present through observing, responding, and selectively intervening when situations arise.
9. Be physically and emotionally present during struggles, disputes, and conflicts between toddlers.

Types of Play:

Solitary Play: Toddler plays alone with objects.

Parallel Play: Two toddlers play side-by-side occasionally glancing at each other.

Associative Play: Two toddlers play side-by-side and may initiate each other's or incorporate the other's play into their own play process.

Cooperative Play: Two toddlers join play to create a happening.

Symbolic Play: Toddlers may use objects in the environment in a way that is different than the purpose of the object (i.e., a broom becomes a horse). It may also be a familiar activity that is performed in a different situation with the proper tools (i.e., feeding a doll at play school with a stick).

Associative Play

Solitary Play

Pikler Institute
Budapest, Hungary

Cooperative Play

Symbolic Play

Parallel Play

Room Environment:

- **Safe** – squat or kneel down and look at the room from the toddler's point of view. Is the room free of harmful hazards 4' to the floor?
- **Clean** – equipment and activities need to be able to be cleaned and disinfected daily with environmentally friendly substances
- **Orderly** – a place for everything and everything in its place in good repair
- **Appropriate** – Developmentally appropriate and varied play objects and materials for different toddler stages
- **Child-size** - furniture and equipment for the toddler to manipulate, carry, and move
- **Space** – sufficient space to create clear pathways
- **Different objects** – varied properties of objects to identify, choose, and manipulate
- **Reality** – depict real lifelike and familiar objects (includes pictures and art in the environment)
- **Representation** – materials that show diversity in family life
- **Climate control** – proper ventilation, heat, air, light, and noise control

Things to Do:

- Observe and be emotionally present
- Calm, peaceful atmosphere
- Traffic and monitor amount of visitation
- Maintain clear ground rules for observers
- Help toddlers care for and about their environment
- Plan for transitions
- Create steps to assist toddlers safely during transitions
- Provide tools to assist in clean up of the classroom
- Be alert and available to handle physical and emotional struggles and disputes before they ignite to conflicts
- Model pro-social behaviors for toddlers

Things to Avoid:

- Zoning out emotionally
- Distractions
- Interruptions
- Loud noise
- Too many people at one time
- Unnecessary visitors
- Messy and chaotic environment
- Unplanned transitions
- Too many transitions
- Herding
- Unnecessary toddler gatherings
- Avoid judgment or demonstrating partiality

Play Object Properties:

- Safe
- Able to pass choke tube test
- Able to be cleaned
- Varied in size, shape, color, weight, texture, and function
- Able to be manipulated and carried by toddler
- Represent cognitive, social, emotional, language, and diversity awareness

Indoor Objects:

Dolls, balls, puzzles, small figures of family, farm and domestic animal representations, cars, blocks, Lego's, manipulatives, dramatic play objects, easel and paints, large gross motor structures, water and sand table, sorting box, tractors, books, bead stringing, musical instruments, kitchen setup with objects, and objects representing cause and effect (i.e. tracking devices).

Outdoor Objects:

Sandbox and sand toys, large trucks, poppers, bikes, trikes, picnic tables, shade, large gross motor structures, art supplies (easel, paint, etc.), blocks, water table and objects, and balls.

Adult Role:

1. Prepare, observe, and monitor the play environment.
2. Check equipment daily for safety, broken and missing pieces, and debris.
3. Evaluate appropriateness of objects and activities.
4. Maintain and clean play equipment.
5. Be available to intervene around safety when necessary.
6. Observe and respond to caregiving as needed.
7. Observe play activities to evaluate needs and wants.
8. Allow choice and free movement for toddlers.
9. Be available for physical and emotional needs.
10. Respond to struggles, disputes, and conflicts between toddlers.
11. During conflict; move close, reflect, and sportscast what you see happening non-judgmentally.
12. Model appropriate behaviors and pro-social behaviors/skills for toddlers.
13. Use language to describe what is happening between toddlers.

Language

Rationale:

Language experiences and activities need to be a large part of the toddler curriculum. Toddlers need many rich language experiences with adults to learn to understand and communicate. Through language, toddlers are able to express themselves and acquire important skills as they relate with others. A variety of language activities needs to be available in the toddler classroom organized on shelves for toddlers to choose, engage, and learn. Books, songs, fingerplays, and music with one child, a small group of children, and the entire toddler community should occur throughout the day. When toddlers experience active communication with peers and adults, they are able to associate words and their meanings. Communicating with others helps to make necessary connections that promote positive skills in language development and expression. Adults can offer a variety of rich language opportunities through their everyday care routines. Adults need to interact with toddlers in interesting and interactive language activities.

Goals:

- To provide a rich language environment that assists toddler language comprehension, expression, and skills
- To dialogue with toddlers about what is happening during caregiving (i.e. toileting)
- To provide language experiences that enrich toddlers' language development (stories, songs, finger plays, music, labeling, naming objects, asking questions to toddlers, etc.)
- To create appropriate language activities that represent a variety of materials and objects to build language skills (musical instruments, books, figures of pets, farm, and zoo animals, figures of people, matching familiar objects, and pictures of fruits and vegetables, etc.)
- To express varied, soothing, animated, and exaggerated tones when engaged in songs and music activities
- To speak in clear, short, concise sentences when dialoguing with toddlers
- To wait for toddlers to process information before responding
- To ask inquiring questions with toddlers as a way to expand thoughts and extend language expression

Language Support Materials

1. Variety of factual books that represent real images/objects
2. Soft, quiet reading area away from high traffic areas
3. Language objects (i.e., telephones, photos, puzzles, and puppets)
4. Interesting musical instruments
5. Tape or CD player
6. Dolls that offer a range of cultural diversity
7. Various categories of animals (pet, farm, zoo, etc.), matching objects, fruits, vegetables, etc.
8. Matching object to object and object to picture activities (for older toddlers).
9. Classification (table setting, transportation, etc.)
10. Magnets on a metal tray to match
11. Mystery bag game to play with an adult
12. Naming objects in the classroom
13. Variation textures (rough, smooth, etc.)
14. Dramatic play objects, i.e., dress up
15. Full length mirror
16. Representation of familiar and real objects
17. Pictures on the wall at the toddler's eye level
18. Gatherings for language activity times

Language Development 18-36 months:

Self-talk: talk about what you see, hear, and are doing.

Parallel talk: dialogue about what you see, hear and about what the child is doing.

- Comment about what the toddler is telling you.
- Fill in left out words.
- Tell what is going to happen.
- Assist by labeling and naming objects.
- Ask questions to expand thoughts.

Holophrastic Speech: (first use of words) naming words (i.e. specific parts of the body); specific names (i.e., mama); action words (i.e., bye-bye).

Locutionary Speech: (18-24 months) sentences as in adult speech; simple sentences with conventional meaning; 50 word vocabulary.

Note:

Toddlers have an explosion of language in which their vocabulary expands to 200 words. They begin to use pronouns (singular and plural), sing songs, recite rhymes, and start to have 2-3 word sentences. Telegraphic speech emerges with whole sentence replaced by noun-action, i.e. baby sleep, "I do").

Expressive Language Evaluation Scale:

18-21 months:

- Minimum vocabulary 10 words
- Names objects when shown (i.e., doll, ball)
- Names pictures of familiar objects (i.e., dog, shoe)
- Asks for wants (i.e., milk)
- Leaves off beginning and end of phrases, common expression, "all gone"

21-24 months:

- Minimum vocabulary of 20 words
- Combines two or three words that express different ideas (i.e. mommy go bye-bye)
- Expressive vocabulary of 25 words mostly nouns, some verbs
- Spontaneously uses names of familiar objects
- Talks in short 2-3 word sentences

24-30 months:

- Vocabulary may exceed 50 words
- Uses pronoun "I"
- Three word sentences
- Verbalizes immediate experiences
- Asks for another (i.e. cookie)
- Understands the concept of what, where and who

30-36 months:

- Gives full name of objects to include self
- Well-formed, simple sentences
- Common expression, "I did it"
- Refers to self by pronoun rather than by name
- Speech activities are repetitive
- Can name 8 pictures correctly (i.e. cup, kitty, shoe, etc.)
- Knows if they are a boy or girl
- Uses some plurals
- Tells action of picture (i.e. baby is sleeping, daddy wash car)
- Understands the concept of how and when

Early Literacy Checklist

Provide the following materials to increase early literacy as the toddlers grow and develop. Once a literacy item has been introduced to the child, you don't need to remove it. A literacy area should grow to include both the familiar and interesting new items that support the children's level of language development.

18-36 months:

- A book display, easily accessible, at the child's eye level and reach
- Books with colorful pictures, short stories, and tactile representation
- Child sized table and chairs
- Drumming, strumming, and sound producing musical instruments
- Repetitive, sing-along, interactive songs and finger plays
- Matching games
- Puppets, dolls, and a dollhouse
- Puzzles with easy grasp handles; 4-8 pieces depending on skill and development
- Large unlined paper, fat crayons, large chalk, play dough, paint, scissors, beads, fabric, and other art mediums
- A variety of plastic or wooden blocks for stacking and building
- Dress up items such as clothes, shoes, hats, purses, and jewelry
- Full length mirror for dramatic play
- Props such as phones, magazines, dolls, kitchen sets, and utensils
- Water and sand play with objects
- Moving toys such as cars, boats, wagons, etc.

Toddler Curriculum Activities

Rationale:

Toddlers learn best by experiencing a stable relationship with an adult they know and trust. Toddlers learn by using their whole bodies and senses to gain information from peers, objects, and activities they choose in their environment. When giving toddlers care, it is important to include them in the process by allowing them to participate for their ability and development. Adults need to be sensitive to the way toddlers gain information and knowledge. For example, toddlers learn by "doing" and having hands-on experiences. It is also important to be aware that each toddler has personal preferences. Allowing them freedom to move and choose as they interact in their environment prevents many power struggles with toddlers. These experiences assist them to discover and concentrate on what is of interest to them. Speaking in clear, short sentences, giving time, and waiting for toddlers to process helps them gain competency in understanding what is occurring as they relate to what is happening.

Goals:

- To provide a rich environment that relates to all developmental areas of learning (physical, cognitive, linguistic, social, emotional)
- To allow toddlers to move freely and choose objects and activities of their interest
- To allow toddlers to develop concentration by providing time for them to stay involved in their activity of interest
- To assist toddlers in self-help skills by allowing them to participate in the care of self and their environment
- To respect each toddler as a unique individual who has the right to express himself
- To set safe limits for toddlers to relate with each other
- To model social and emotional behaviors that foster respectful and empathetic responses towards others

How to Constitute a Specific Toddler Curriculum

1. Language Arts

Goals:

- To provide a language environment with many activities to choose from
- To allow toddlers to choose activities that address their language interests as well as meet their developmental needs

Environmental Support and Equipment:

2 shelves

Bookcase with books in good repair

Small soft chair, pillow, mat, etc.

Rug for gathering the group

Real life pictures on walls

Varied books in good repair

Puzzles

Musical instruments

Animal objects

Object cards (fruits, vegetables, transportation, etc.)

Teacher made activities (books of shapes, color, animals, etc.)

Baskets to place activities in

Note:

Check shelves daily to make sure activities are complete, in good order and repair (if necessary).

Sample Language Shelf:

Shelf sequence moves from left to right, simple to more complex, and concrete to abstract, top to bottom.

- Objects
- Object to object
- Object to picture
- Picture
- Picture to picture

2. Manipulative Activities

Goals:

- To provide ample floor space away from quiet areas (i.e. language, reading corner) to allow toddlers to choose their objects of play.
- To provide a variety of manipulatives
- To assist toddlers to place objects back on the shelf where they belong

Environmental Support and Equipment

Shelf
Rug to delineate space
Legos
Wood blocks
Peg board
Shape blocks
Lacing shapes
Puzzles
Nesting blocks
1-5 ring counter
Shape sorter
Sensory blocks
Lock box
Baskets to place activities in
A variety of large and small containers

Note:

Various properties of objects that show variation of size, shape, color, texture, and weight need to be included in the manipulative area. Clean and check area to make sure all pieces are in good repair.

3. Care of Self and Environment

Goals:

- To allow children to learn to care for, respect and appreciate their bodies while developing self-help skills
- To help toddlers learn to care for their environment

Note on care of self:

Assist toddlers in care of self. Allow toddlers to get own diaper and help in the toilet process. Demonstrate to toddler and help toddler learn how to blow nose, wash hands, clean up after snack. Care of self activities need a special designated place that remains constant in the environment. Other self-care activities include helping to dress, undress self, hand washing, brushing teeth. It is essential for all necessary items to be in the specific area for care of self to be successful.

Note on care of environment:

Have necessary tools and items in readiness for toddlers to help care for the environment. Allow toddlers to water plants, sweep, dust shelves, wipe and mop spills. Remind toddlers to push in chairs and return activities to proper place on shelf when finished. Have a designated place for clean-up tools.

Environmental Support and Equipment:

Mop
Broom
Sponges
Toothbrushes
Nose blowing items such as Kleenex, trash can, mirror, etc.

Activities to include in care of environment:

- Plant watering
- Mopping
- Dusting
- Sweeping
- Help to feed and care for animal
- Window washing

4. Self-paced Snack (optional depending on skill level)

Goals:

- To allow toddlers to have a pleasurable eating experience
- To allow toddlers to select own snack for eating and sit peacefully with other toddlers while eating
- To help develop skills that include hand washing, pouring, scooping, sitting at table with others, pulling out and pushing in chair, cleaning up after themselves, washing a glass

Environmental Support and Equipment

Designated snack area near a water source
Glasses
Snack bowl
Scoop
Wash cloths
Bibs (Optional)
Table
Chair
Shelf
Trash can
Food items

Basic rules:

To wash hands before eating
To sit while eating
To sit peacefully with other children (not to exceed 4)
To eat what toddler has selected
To be respectful of others and their food
To clean up after self
To push in and pull out chair

5. Art Activities (individual and/or small group depending on toddler preference)

Goals:

- To allow toddlers to select individual art experience of his/her choice from the art shelf
- To provide small group art experiences with 2-4 children monitored by an adult

Environmental Support and Equipment:

Paint
Chalk
Glue
Playdough with tools
Crayons
Paper
Easel
Aprons

Note on care of environment:

Provide individual activity for painting, chalking, gluing, coloring, and play dough on shelf. Have available apron for toddlers to put on during art projects. Observe toddlers to see when, if, and how to be available for assistance (i.e., may need to help put on an apron). Provide a small group art activity such as painting on a large butcher paper with 2-3 colored paints. Select different projects and mediums throughout the week.

6. Dramatic Experience

Goals:

- To allow toddlers to experience opportunities to express themselves in different types of play (i.e., symbolic-pretend play)
- To provide a separate designated area to support dramatic play

Environmental Support and Equipment

Mirror

Hats, gloves, slippers, shoes, bracelets, capes, etc.

Dolls

Housekeeping sink, stove, refrigerator (wood)

Dishes, cups, and kitchen utensils

7. Gross Motor and Large Motor Activities

Goals:

- To allow toddlers opportunities for fine motor and large muscle movement throughout their day
- To provide equipment for toddlers to experience maximum effort of their bodies

Environmental Support and Equipment:

- Large motor structure with ramp, slide, steps, platform
- Objects that allow for maximum effort (i.e., large jugs for carrying filled with various weighted substances)
- Tracking devices
- Bean bag toss
- Sit and spin apparatus
- Balance beam

8. Outdoor Experiences

Goals:

- To provide rich sensory experiences for children
- To allow toddlers opportunities to experience the outdoor classroom
- To provide opportunities to promote rich social and creative play
- To stimulate all aspects of development

Environmental Support and Equipment:

- Outdoor area with direct or easy access from the classroom
- A variety of natural surfaces and materials such as grass, woodchips, stones, and dirt
- Loose parts (such as logs and leaves)
- Dramatic play materials (hats, dishes, kitchen accessories)
- Sensory rich plants such as thyme, lemon grass, and moss

Discipline and Classroom Management

Rationale:

Discipline means "to follow" and needs to reflect a positive approach with clear alternatives when intervening. Discipline for toddlers is a way for them to learn what is expected and how to get along with others in their environment. When toddlers experience appropriate guidelines, they feel safe and better able to feel secure and achieve self-regulation. Setting limits for toddlers assists them to gain pro-social skills that help the toddler learn how to be with others in respectful and peaceful ways. Clear, consistent rules that are safe and simple to understand help the toddler to behave as they relate in their environment and with others.

Goals:

- To design a safe environment for toddlers to experience
- To help toddlers learn acceptable ways of relating to peers and adults they encounter
- To set few, clear, safe and consistent house rules
- To guide toddlers through the experiences of relating to others
- To set developmentally appropriate guidelines that help toddlers to cooperate
- To develop predictable routines toddlers can rely on and trust
- To create simple transitions with signals that alert toddlers for change
- To give ample time for toddlers to process and react to information

Process – without struggle, preventative measures:

- Make sure your environment is safe for the youngest child in your classroom.
- Provide a variety of rich hands-on activities and experiences that promote inquiry, discovery, and problem solving skills.
- Add mediums like water and sand to the environment daily.
- Limit number of children who can do a specific activity (i.e., you need an apron to do water play. Both aprons are being used right now, how about ...while you wait.
- Develop language areas with a variety of puzzles, books, matching cards, animals, etc.
- Establish and maintain few simple appropriate house rules for toddlers (i.e., walking feet in classroom).

- Have the same consistent rules for all children.
- Observe and monitor children's social encounters.
- Offset beginning potential conflicts by offering suggestions, redirection, or positioning yourself close to the child

Process – during struggle or conflict

1. Observe when two toddlers are beginning to struggle or dispute.
2. Move in closer to the toddlers.
3. Wait to see what is happening, many toddlers will stop the dispute when an adult moves closer.
4. When toddlers persist, remain calm, non-judgmental, and emotionally present.
5. Offer options (i.e., Johnny, did you see there is another red car?) and wait to see the reaction.
6. Sportscast when appropriate "Karami, Michael really wants the red car you have in your hands." Wait. "Michael, can you tell Kamari that you had the car and want it?
7. Provide time for the toddlers to process this new information.
8. Give options, choices, and negotiation skills for the toddlers to use (i.e., "If you look by the chair Johnny, you will find another red car.").
9. Provide safety to both toddlers throughout the experience.
10. Remain neutral and non-judgmental regarding the outcome.
11. Be the second person to leave the situation. In other words, stay near the children until one of them walks away.

Steps to remember (observe throughout process):

1. Move close.
2. Monitor safety of all children involved.
3. Offer suggestions and/or options.
4. Remain calm.
5. Be nonjudgmental and uninvested in outcome.
6. Sportscast what you see happening.
7. Stay emotionally present and attentive.
8. Give time for toddlers to work it out.
9. Be second to leave the situation.

Note:

When a toddler is out of control and is having a temper tantrum that requires adult intervention, take the child to a quiet area of the room or outdoors. Stay with the child until he reaches a state of calm and is able to reenter the environment. Be sure before you begin that you tell the child you are going to move him and be with him until he can be safe again.

General Classroom Strategies:

Make sure the discipline measure

1. Is appropriate to the stage of the child.
2. Is specific and focused on particular behavior.
3. Is immediate to what happened.
4. Is consistent each time.
5. Is underscored with language.
6. Gives a rationale to why behavior is not acceptable.
7. Models appropriate behavior.
8. Gives concrete options and alternatives.
9. Acknowledges feelings.
10. Clarifies what is appropriate.
11. Offers reasonable choice options.
12. Gives the behavior you want to see happen ("Feet on floor").
13. Refrains from making judgment statements about the child ("you're being naughty when you hit").
14. Provides child opportunities to self regulate.
15. Gives verbal feedback to child.
16. Provides opportunities for trial and error.
17. Is respectful of the child while interacting.
18. Provides opportunities for redirection.

Environmental Design

Rationale:

A safe child friendly environment that the toddler can relate to is essential to his maturation and learning process. The role of the adult to design, implement, and maintain the environment for the toddler to express his needs and abilities is important to his well-being at the center. When the environment is set up to meet the needs of the toddler on all developmental domains of learning (physical, cognitive, linguistic, social, and emotional) toddlers stay focused, interested, active, and content. The environment for toddlers needs to provide ways they can express their abilities and interests. For example, toddlers have a need to move their whole bodies frequently, therefore the room needs to have clear pathways, a large motor structure (as well as access to outdoors if possible) and defined areas for a variety of learning activities. At the same time, toddlers like to experience a variety of manipulatives to develop their fine motor skills. These can be displayed in baskets placed neatly on shelves or in the manipulative area. Placing items in the same place on the shelf helps the toddler remember where to place the activity when he is finished. Encouraging the toddler to help care for his environment allows him to feel ownership as well as demonstrate his self-help skills. Modeling and showing the toddler ways to be helpful supports his initiation and regulation. A variety of mediums, to include sand, water, and art activities need to be available on a daily basis to support his need to experience several kinds of mediums.

Goals:

- To design and create a safe environment that meets needs and interests of toddlers
- To have a variety of art activities that the toddler can choose to experience
- To care for and maintain the environment daily
- To make sure there is enough child size tables, chairs, and other large equipment for the number of children in the classroom
- To disinfect the room daily and check and replenish equipment as needed to stay in good repair
- To observe and add more complexity to the materials as the children grow and develop (i.e., changing puzzle to more complex 6-9 piece)
- To soften the room with fabric, rugs, and plants
- To insure the safety of the room and avoid developing corners or nooks where you cannot see children
- To define learning areas by developing specific spaces and coordinating activities based on active vs. quiet areas, etc.
- To offer a variety of activities, objects, and manipulatives that toddlers can explore, discover, and create

Note:

Set up the room based on toddler needs and interests (be sure to observe your room with children in it to see what is working and what needs to be changed). Place child friendly furniture in areas that use tables and chairs (i.e., art area, language area, snack area). Make sure that art and snack areas are positioned close to the water source. Be sure the physical care environments (like toileting) have ample room to support adult and child interactions. Be sure all personal items are readily accessible so as not to deflect the relationship during toileting. In all the curriculum areas, be sure appropriate items are available for the adult and the child to be successful in that space.

Elements that comprise appropriate environments (including but not limited to):

1. **Healthy** - few chances to become infected with disease or illness (i.e., maintain good handwashing techniques)
2. **Safe** - able to move around room safely with few "no's" from adult. Go onto your knees to observe room 4' down for safety
3. **Comfortable** - for adults and children to have equipment that is appropriate and manageable to their sizes and the climate is peaceful with busy but productive noise level
4. **Convenient** - able to see, find, and manipulate play objects on their own and replace when finished
5. **Child size** - able to manipulate and use their environment because equipment is scaled to their size and designed for their use
6. **Flexible** - able to change and expand with the growing needs of the children. Able to change and arrange spaces to shift activities and interests (back down or expand a particular activity)
7. **Movement** - able to move through space at their own volition have option for large and fine motor movement
8. **Choice** - opportunity to explore and choose activities of their interest in their own time and way

The environment needs to be able to:

1. Develop toddlers' initiative, self-help, and self-regulation as well as their growing need for independence.
2. Have structure, order and defined spaces, "a place for everything and everything in it's place".
3. Support the ability of the child to place items where they belong.

4. Depict reality (i.e., fine art, pictures that represent true images, etc.)
5. Have many sensorial experiences.
6. Provide natural elements like plants, animals, etc.
7. Be aesthetically pleasing and beautiful. The design of the room and activities needs to be simple, natural quality, and attractively displayed.
8. Allow the caregiver to be the keeper of the room, ever observant and watchful to what is needed for the toddlers learning and well-being.

Questions on Environment

1. Write down five words which best describe your view of environments for infants and toddlers.

2. Write down three things that are essential for infant and toddler environments.

3. If I were going to change one thing in my environment, it would be:

4. When I enter my classroom, I get a feeling of:

5. If I had my way, my environment for infants and toddlers would...

6. The best advice I could give my infant and toddler parents regarding the environment is:

Parents as Partners for Infants

Rationale:

Babies learn how to relate through experiences with significant adults (i.e. parents, relatives, caregivers). Parents need healthy caregiving models they can rely on and trust to assist them in learning how to care for their babies. Caregivers are valuable resources in providing support to parents as they develop parenting skills. When caregivers understand the families' culture and respect differences in their parent population, valuable alliances can occur that provide information about babies. Parents are the first teachers of their child and are important in providing information helpful to caregivers who are trying to give responsive and individualized care. Keeping channels of communication open through contact and meaningful dialogue allows valuable knowledge to be exchanged that supports the ongoing relationship between caregivers and parents. These relationships help to foster and maintain the health and well-being of babies in group care.

Goals:

- Support parent skills and foster their confidence.
- Keep lines of communication open.
- Model language in caregiving and activities for parents.
- Recognize each other's knowledge and role.
- Help identify issues and create appropriate resources for parents.
- Share in the decision making process.
- Understand culture and diversity of individual families.

Process:

Parents and caregivers benefit by maintaining a close relationship with one another. This relationship is built on continued positive experiences. These experiences need to relate to infant growth and development, care and well-being of their baby, as well as, positive parenting styles.

1. Model sensitive and responsive care routine to parents.
2. Be available to talk about issues and/or concerns of parents.
3. Support infant development by allowing parents to observe their infants for brief periods of time.
4. Dialogue about observations with parents.
5. Support the teachable moment for parents through caregiving routines.
6. Help parents understand the philosophy of care that you provide for the baby.
7. Make connections with parents so they can follow through continuity of care at home.

Caregiver Self- Reflection:

1. How do you feel about working with families?
2. What do you most like about relating with families?
3. What do you need to work on in relations with families?
4. What are your strengths in working with families?
5. What do you find most difficult when relating to families?

Objectives of Infant Pedagogy

1. To ensure the quality of life and well being of all infants placed in the infant development center
2. For the adult caregiver to promote and maintain a primary care relationship with a small group of infants
3. To provide individual care in a timely fashion to each infant, based on need and sensitive observations of infant cues
4. To develop a participating and cooperative relationship with families

Parents as Partners for Toddlers

Rationale:

Toddlers are scientists who are actively moving as they explore and discover within their environment. Emotionally, they are in a push-pull struggle between dependency and interdependency with significant adults. It is important for the adult to read cues to determine when the toddler is seeking help and when he wants to do it by himself. The young toddler exhibits many different emotions in a brief period of time. This can exhaust and perplex an adult. For parents, it is important for them to maintain a safe home environment with few clear and simple rules that toddlers can understand. Helping parents to develop management strategies that are consistent, and routines that are predictable (especially sleep routines) will aid parents and diminish frustration and confusion.

Goals:

- To be open and receptive in communicating with parents
- To recognize and respect parent knowledge and role as primary teacher
- To support parent confidence
- To identify and support parent's needs
- To create a support system as a resource
- To collaborate with parents regarding decisions
- To understand parent's culture and accept diversity
- To help parents define appropriate guidelines for toddler safety and limit setting

Process:

1. Share information with parents regarding their child.
2. Discuss and model appropriate behaviors for parents to use in setting limits.
3. Help parents identify emotions and feelings their toddler evokes in them.
4. Help parents to use appropriate control of their feelings and remain peaceful and calm when feeling frustrated or angry.
5. Encourage parents to assist toddlers in self-care routines at home to allow toddlers to develop their abilities (i.e., self-paced snack, participatory toileting).
6. Discuss language opportunities that parents can use in relating to their toddler at home.
7. Develop a professional partnership with parents that encourages them to support toddler activities in their home environment.

Caregiver Self Reflection

1. How do you feel about working with the toddler parents?

2. What do you like about working with parents? Toddlers?

3. How do you see yourself being helpful with parents?

4. What do you need to work on to be more available and successful in supporting parents?

Developmental Characteristics of Babies 1 month to 18 months

	1-4 Months	4-8 Months
PHYSICAL	• Moves from reflex to more purposeful movement • Holds head up • Moves from side to side • May roll over • Studies hands • Brings objects to mouth • Reaches for objects	• Moves intentionally • Begins to develop eye-hand coordination • Discovers feet • Rolls onto stomach from back and from back to stomach • Moves toward what he or she sees and hears • May sit up or crawl • Transfers objects from hand to hand
COGNITIVE	• Visually tracks an object • Shows a preference for a family member—able to recognize who and what belongs in the environment • Looks at the mouth of person speaking • Gazes at objects • Curious—shows interest in environment	• Distinguishes different properties of objects • Solves simple problems • Holds the idea of something in his or her brain (object permanence) • Repeats actions • Moves intentionally
SOCIAL-EMOTIONAL	• Laughs socially • Smiles interactively • Responds to familiar voices • Smiles after recognizing someone • Is responsive to attention	• Explores his or hers environment • Initiates social interactions • Develops stranger anxiety • Shows resistance—begins to develop his or her will • Has goal-directed behaviors • Expresses emotions (happy, sad, anxious, and so on) • Smiles broadly • Looks for reactions on the faces of others
LANGUAGE	• Coos • Makes "raspberries" • Makes sounds	• Babbles • May say "ma ma" or "da da" • Develops more selective hearing • Understands gestures • Starts to communicate with other infants or shows interest in doing so

Developmental Characteristics of Babies 1 month to 18 months

	8-12 Months	12-18 Months
PHYSICAL	• Creeps • Sits up • Stoops • Pivots • Pulls up, cruises • May walk • Grasps objects of choice and releases them • Dumps • Throws	• Walks alone • Explores his or her environment • Climbs • Opens and closes objects • Uses tools, such as a spoon • Carries objects when walking • Uses a pincer grip
COGNITIVE	• Recognizes his or her name and the names of familiar objects • Has memory—begins to remember people, events and objects • Holds a concept in his or her mind • Thinks symbolically • Has comprehension—begins to understand simple commands, a few words, and body gestures • Understands two- and three-word sentences • Acts intentionally	• Loves opposites • Identifies objects and pictures • Practices trial and error • Repeats actions • Understands that objects have names • Is interested in cause and effect • Responds to commands or request • Returns to activity of interest
SOCIAL-EMOTIONAL	• Anticipates activities • Is emotionally expressive • Anticipates the return of his or her mother, father • Plays more interactively with others (peek-a-boo)	• Is enthusiastic • Shows excitement and elation • Loves an audience • Begins to hold back anger • Insists on his or her own way • Is a watchful observer • Is very interested in peers
LANGUAGE	• Begins to understand that words have meaning • Says first intentional word • Imitates sounds and vocalizations • Demonstrates symbolic hand gestures	• May say "please" • Mimics actions • Names objects • Repeats animal sounds • May use some words to communicate • Absorbs language and tries to communicate

Developmental Characteristics of Babies 18 month to 24 months

	18-24 Months	24-36 Months
PHYSICAL	• Kicks, throws, climbs, runs • Developing hand-eye coordination and pincer grasp • Holds implements such as paint brush, crayon, chalk • Can undress self • 18 primary teeth	• Can be successful at toilet learning • Has full movement: jumping, skipping • Expands maximum effort, carries heavy objects, takes long walks, exercises and perfects large muscles • Can ride a three-wheeled bike • Can dress self • Enjoys climbing • Pincer grasp
COGNITIVE	• Beginning of thoughts • Can hold a symbol in their head and think symbolically • Carries memory of significant adults • Responds to strangers • Misses parent • Begins playing make-believe • Not easily distracted • Egocentric - cannot see other's point of view • Deductive reasoning	• Begins to distinguish between reality and make-believe • Can remember sequences in routines • Can discriminate size and shape • Can categorize • Understands instructions • Can draw a circle • Begins to understand cause and effect relationships • Integrates themes into play
SOCIAL-EMOTIONAL	• Shows awareness of other's feelings • Shows affection to parent with smiles, hugs, and kisses • Can express feelings • Increased awareness of separation combined with awareness of vulnerability • Can direct adult • Proud of accomplishments • Strong sibling rivalry • Separation anxiety • Parallel play • Can be oppositional • Needs limits • Will test boundaries	• Can play happily alone but loves an audience • Understands autonomy but resists • Needs limits • Begins to be able to reason about feelings • Age of conflict between dependency and interdependency • Push/pull struggles • Moving towards sharing • Loves chores; wants to help • Engages in cooperative as well as parallel play • Accepts reasonable limits • Pretend play with others • Emerging friendships
LANGUAGE	• Language explosion; says about 200 words • 2-3 word sentences • Can follow 2 simple directions at a time • Has comprehension; can respond to questions • Can carry on a conversation • Uses I when referring to self • Imitates vocal inflections • Intentional communication	• Can learn songs; likes rhyming • Makes more complex sentences • Uses plurals, nouns, verbs, adjectives, adverbs, and prepositions • Describes/asks questions • Intrigued by whispering • Repeats stories and games

Ainsworth, M., Bell, S., & Stayton, D. (1974). Infant-Mother Attachment and Social Development and Socialization as a Product of Reciprocal Responsiveness to Signals. Cambridge, UK: University Press.

Bayer, C., Whaley, K., & May, S. (1995). Strategic Assistance in Toddler Disputes: II. Sequences and Patterns of Teachers' Message Strategies. Early Education and Development, 6 (4), 405-432.

Brazelton, T. (1992). Touchpoints: Your Child's Emotional and Behavioral Development. New York: Addison-Wesley Publishing Company.

Bredekamp, S., & Copple, C. (1997). Developmentally Appropriate Practice in Early Childhood Programs. Washington, D.C.: NAEYC.

Butterfield, P., Martin, C., & Prarie, A. (2004). Emotional Connections. Washington, D.C.: Zero to Three Press.

Christie, T. (2011). Respect. Wellington, New Zealand: Childspace Early Childhood Institute.

Crain, W. (2011). Theories of Development. New York: Prentice Hall.

DaRos-Voseles, D., & Kovach, B. (1998). Toddlers and Caregivers During Conflict. Childhood Education, 75(1), 25-30.

David, M., & Appell, G. (2001). An Unusual Approach to Mothering. Budapest: Pikler-Loczy Tarsasag.

Eliot, L. (1999). What's Going on in There? New York: Bantam

Elliot, E. (2003). Helping a Baby Adjust to Center Care. Young Children, 58(4), 22-28.

Erikson, E. (1950). Childhood and Society (2nd ed.). New York: W.W. Norton and Company.

Falk, J. (2011). Why the prone position should not be used for young infants. Official Journal of Hungarian Pediatrics Association, Supplement A(Child and Youth Medical Journal).

Falk, J. (1994). Forty Years of Loczy. Sensory Awareness Foundation Bulletin, 14, 38-46.

Falk, J., & Pikler, E. (1972). Data on adult outcomes of the social adjustment of children reared in the Pikler Institute. Magysr Pszichologiai Szemle, 29(3-4), 488-500.

Foreman, G., & Kuschner, D. (1983). The Child's Construction of Knowledge: Piaget for Teaching Children. Washington, D.C.: NAEYC.

Frailberg, S. (1959). The Magic Years. New York: Simon and Shuster.

Gerber, M. (1998). Dear Parent: Caring for Infants with Respect (2nd ed.). Los Angeles: Resources for Infant Educarers

Gerber, M. & Johnson, A. (1998). Your Self-Confident Baby. New York: John Wiley and Sons.

Gerber, M. (1979). The RIE Manual for Parents and Professionals. Los Angeles: Resources for Infant Educarers.

Gerber, M., & Forrest, T. (Writers). (1978). On Their Own With Our Help. In RIE (Producer): Resources for Infant Educarers.

Ginsburg, H., & Opper, S. (1969). Piaget's Theory of Intellectual Development: An Introduction. Englewood Cliffs, New Jersey: Prentice-Hall.

Golse, B. (2010). Observation, application and research: The Pikler paradigm. The Signal: Newsletter of the World Association for Infant Mental Health, 18(3-4), 15.

Gonzalez-Mena, J. (2004). What can an orphanage teach us? Lessons from Budapest. Young Children, 59(5), 26-29.

Gonzalez-Mena, J., Chahin, E., & Briley, L. (2005). The Pikler Institute: A unique way of caring for children. Exchange(November), 49-51.

Gonzalez-Mena, J. & Eyer, D. W. (1993). Infants, toddlers, and caregivers (3rd ed.). Mountain View, Calif.: Mayfield Pub.

Greenspan, S., & Greenspan, N. (1989). First Feelings: Milestones in the Emotional Development of your Baby and Child. New York: Penguin.

Honig, A. (2002). Secure Relationships: Nurturing Infant-Toddler Attachment in Early Care Settings. Washington, D.C.: NAEYC.

Howes, C. (1998). Continuity of care: The importance of infant, toddler, caregiver relationships. Zero to Three, 18(6), 7-11.

Kallo, E., & Balog, G. (2005). The Origins of Free Play. Budapest: Pikler-Loczy Tarsasag.

Resources and Readings

Katz, L., & McClellen, D. (1997). Fostering Children's Social Competence: The Teacher's Role. Waashington, D.C.: NAEYC.

Keren, M. (2010). Can an institution really be a growth promoting environment?. The Signal: Newsletter of the World Association for Infant Mental Health, 18(3-4), 25.

Konicheckis, A. (2010). Being in movement. The Signal: Newsletter of the World Association for Infant Mental Health, 18(3-4), 5-6.

Kovach, B., & DaRos-Voseles, D. (1995). The use of language as rationale for respectful and reciprocal caregiving with infants. Montessori Life, 7(2), 16-17.

Kovach, B., & DaRos-Voseles, D. (1998). Respectful, individual, and responsive caregiving of infants: The key to succesful care in group settings. Young Children, 53(3), 61-74.

Kovach, B., & DaRos-Voseles, D. (2008). Being with Babies. Beltsville, MD.: Gryphon House.

Lally, R. (1990). A Guide to Social-Emotional Growth and Socialization. Sacramento: California Department of Education.

Lally, R., & Mangione, P. (2006). The Uniqueness of Infancy Demands a Responsive Approach to Care. Young Children, 67(4), 14-20.

Lieberman, A. (1993). The Emotional Life of the Toddler. New York: The Free Press.

Montessori, M. (1966). The Secret of Childhood. New York: Ballantine Books.

Mooney, C. (2010). Theories of Attachment. St. Paul, Minnesota: Redleaf Press.

Pawl, J. (1990). Infants in day care: Reflections on experiences, expectations, and relationships. Zero to Three: Bulletin of the National Center for Clinical Infant Programs, 1-6.

Petrie, S., & Owen, S. (2006). Authentic Relationships in Group Care for Infants and Toddlers. London: Jessica Kingsley Publishers.

Pikler, E. (1971). Learning of motor skills on the basis of self-induced movements. Exceptional Infant, vol 2., ed. J. Hellmuth, J. 54-89. New York: Bruner/Mazel.

Pikler, E. 1973. Some contributions to the study of gross motor development of children. Child and Adolescent Development, ed. A. Sandovsky, 52-64. New York: Free Press.

Pikler, E. (1978). The Competence of the Infant. Acte Paediatricia Academiae Scientiarum Hungaricae, 20, 185-192.

Pikler, E. (1991) Friedliche Babys – Zufriedene Mütter. Freiburg, Basel, Wien, Herder Verlag. 222 S. (Herder-bücherei.)

Pikler, E. (1993). Excerpts from Peaceful Babies-Contented Mothers. Sensory Awareness Foundation Bulletin, No. 14, Mill Valley, CA.: Sensory Awareness Foundation. pp. 5-24

Pikler, E. (2006). Unfolding of Infants Natural Gross Motor Development. Los Angeles: Resources for Infant Educarers (RIE).

Standing, E. (1957). Maria Montessori: Her Life and Work. New York: American Library.

Stern, D. (1985). The Interpersonal World of the Infant. New York: Basic Books.

Stonehorse, A. (1990). Trusting Toddlers. St. Paul, Minnesota: Red Leaf Press.

Tardos, A. (2007). Bringing Up and Providing Care for Infants and Toddlers in an Institution. Budapest: Pikler-Loczy Tarsasag.

Tardos, A. (2010). The researching infant. The Signal: Newsletter of the World Association for Infant Mental Health, 18(3-4), 9-14.

Tardos, A. (2010). Introducing the Piklerian developmental approach: History and principles. The Signal: Newsletter of the World Association for Infant Mental Health, 18(3-4), 1-4.

Winnicott, D. W. (1965). The Maturational Process and the Facillitating Environment. New York: International Universities Press.

Ziegler, E. (2004). Children's Play: The Roots of Reading. Washington, D.C.: Zero to Three Press.

Pikler/Loczy Fund USA, www.Pikler.org

Pikler-Loczy Association for Young Children, www.pikler.hu

Resources for Infant Educarers, www.rie.org

WestEd/Programs for Infant Toddler Caregivers, www.PITC.org

World Forum On Early Care And Education, see www.WorldForumFoundation.org

Zero to Three, www.zerotothree.org